Muslim Attitudes Towards the European Union

How do Muslim citizens across the globe perceive the European Union? And what factors influence their EU attitudes? This book offers the first systematic theoretical and empirical analysis of Muslim citizens' EU attitudes in and outside the European Union.

Using the best empirical data available, the book demonstrates that Muslim citizens' attitudes are not shaped by their denomination and religious beliefs, but by material and political considerations. It finds that Muslims are most favorable toward the EU due to their positive experiences in European contexts, whereas in contrast, Muslim citizens outside the EU are more skeptical toward the European Union due to sovereignty concerns and the lack of support from the EU and its member states. Such findings not only contribute to the research on social legitimacy of international organizations and international public opinion more generally, but also provide important suggestions for (European) policy makers regarding external and domestic policies.

This book will be of key interest to scholars, students and practitioners of European Union politics, Middle East studies, public opinion and International Relations.

Bernd Schlipphak is Professor for Empirical Methods in the Social Sciences at the Department of Political Science at the University of Münster, Germany. His work has been published in journals such as *The Review of International Organizations, European Union Politics*, the *Journal of Common Market Studies* and the *Journal of European Public Policy*.

Mujtaba Ali Isani is a Post-Doctoral Fellow at the Department of Political Science at the University of Münster, Germany. His work has been published in the *Journal of Common Market Studies, Political Research Quarterly, International Political Science Review* and *European Union Politics*.

Routledge Advances in European Politics

Dynamics of Political Change in Ireland
Making and breaking a divided island
Edited by Niall Ó Dochartaigh, Katy Hayward and Elizabeth Meehan

European Enlargement across Rounds and Beyond Borders
Edited by Haakon A. Ikonomou, Aurélie Andry, and Rebekka Byberg

Uncovering the Territorial Dimension of European Union Cohesion Policy
Cohesion, development, impact assessment, and cooperation
Edited by Eduardo Medeiros

The Crisis of the European Union
Challenges, analyses, solutions
Edited by Andreas Grimmel

Promoting National Priorities in EU Foreign Policy
Czech Republic and the EU
Tomáš Weiss

Italy from Crisis to Crisis
Political economy, security, and society in the 21st century
Matthew Evangelista

Lobbying Success in the European Union
The role of information and frames
Daniel Rasch

Muslim Attitudes Towards the European Union
Bernd Schlipphak and Mujtaba Ali Isani

For a full list of titles in this series, please visit www.routledge.com

Muslim Attitudes Towards the European Union

Bernd Schlipphak and
Mujtaba Ali Isani

Routledge
Taylor & Francis Group

LONDON AND NEW YORK

First published 2019 by Routledge

2 Park Square, Milton Park, Abingdon, Oxfordshire OX14 4RN

52 Vanderbilt Avenue, New York, NY 10017

Routledge is an imprint of the Taylor & Francis Group, an informa business

First issued in paperback 2020

British Library Cataloguing-in-Publication Data
A catalogue record for this book is available from the British Library

Library of Congress Cataloging-in-Publication Data
A catalog record has been requested for this book

ISBN: 978-1-138-60705-7 (hbk)
ISBN: 978-0-367-67043-6 (pbk)

Typeset in Times New Roman
by Apex CoVantage, LLC

Contents

Figures and tables

Figures

Tables

Preface

This book is a product of our research project on "Foreign States and International Organization in the Perception of the Arab Publics" at the University of Muenster's Excellence Cluster on "Religion and Politics" (A2-24). The initial puzzle that motivates this book is empirical in nature: Arab Muslims are shown to be less favorable of international and regional organizations such as the European Union (EU). Does this mean that *all* Muslims share similar (negative) feelings toward the European Union? And the second obvious question that follows is: what mechanisms and factors help us analyze Muslim attitudes?

We think that these are pertinent and important questions to answer not only for research on attitudes toward the EU but also for the general comprehension of how certain populations such as Muslims develop their opinion toward certain international actors. Given also a renewed interest in understanding the behavior of Muslims in the 21st century, especially in Europe after migration of a large number of refugees from the Arab world, we consider this work to address a timely topic bound to invoke the interest of social scientists as well as policy practitioners.

In the book we try to implement a large number of empirical tests for our theoretical model. We then also provide extensive robustness checks to ensure that our results are not artifacts of model choice or the consequence of the use a particular empirical method. We also think that this definitely also is not the final word on the topic. There is great room for more, quality empirical research on the topic, especially research that takes into account the country-level variation in public attitudes toward international actors.

Still, the general outlook we present in this book is based on a sound theoretical model and rigorous empirical tests. For the latter, we mainly use large, secondary sources of data such as the Arab Barometer, Pew Global Attitudes and the European Social Survey instead of single-country data that we ourselves collected in the framework of the above-mentioned project. Using these well-known surveys instead allows us to provide a more representative picture, covering a large number of respondents and a diversity of countries. As a result, we are able to offer more generalizable findings than would be the case with data collected within a single or a few countries. As is the case for any secondary use of data, these surveys are not ideal for our research aims. Testing a complex theoretical model of decision making, we have to restrict ourselves at some points to using proxies. Hence, some of the limitations of our empirical findings – which we outline in detail in the respective chapters and in the conclusion – may be due to the unavailability of even better quality data collection.

Still, these surveys are some of the best sources of publicly available data for academic use. Given that we employed extensive robustness checks for our analyses, we are hence confident that our findings provide a general outlook that reliably demonstrates how (Muslim) citizens make up their minds toward the European Union. As the mechanism of developing international attitudes contains both utilitarian and socio-psychological elements, our research shows that the actions of the European Union and domestic actors certainly matter for EU attitudes. Future research – in which we look forward to participate – should therefore take the findings presented in this book as a starting point to analyze more thoroughly the effects of EU external policies on global public opinion.

Acknowledgments

Finalizing this book, we are grateful to a large number of persons and institutions. Most importantly, we thank Routledge – and especially Andrew Taylor and Sophie Iddamalgoda – for not only providing us with the opportunity to present our innovative theoretical concepts and the large number of empirical tests in the format of this book but also for their supportive, rapid and understanding way of managing the whole publication process. In addition, we are very grateful to SAGE publishing and John Wiley & Sons for providing us with the opportunity to re-use materials from articles we published earlier in *European Union Politics* and the *Journal of Common Market Studies*. Furthermore, the book would not have been possible without the generous financial support of the research project by the University of Muenster's Excellence Cluster on "Religion and Politics".

When it comes to individuals, we actually do not know where to start as there is a plentitude of helpful persons who provided constructive and valuable feedback throughout the work on the research project. When it comes to general feedback on the relevance of the topic of (Muslim) attitudes toward the European Union, we want especially to thank Karl Kaltenthaler, Gerald Schneider, Dan Silverman and Jan Völkel for constant support and/ or constructive feedback on minor and major questions. Throughout the work on the project, we received valuable comments and – maybe even more importantly – friendly support from Brile Anderson, Natalia Chaban, Lisa Dellmuth, Andreas Dür, Matthias Ecker-Ehrhardt, Benjamin Engst, Will Lowe, Simon Munzert, Christian Rauh, Jonas Tallberg, Ulrich Willems, and a plentitude of anonymous reviewers. In the process of finalizing this book, Nadine Dörffer assisted us in formatting the manuscript.

Introduction

The rational explanation of Muslim attitudes toward the European Union

The European Union (EU) has for long now considered itself to be a 'normative,' 'soft' and 'civil' power (Manners, 2002; Scheipers & Sicurelli, 2007). This self-perception rests on the assumption that the EU has not been violently forcing other states to cooperate or sanctioning others for non-cooperation but has been instead using diplomacy, economic incentives and persuasive rhetoric to convince others. As a result, EU institutions hope for an increased level of social legitimacy around the globe. High levels of public acceptance, such is the calculation, would substantially corroborate with EU economic, development and regional integration policies in other parts of the world.

This self-image received its first blow-back when research on elite opinion toward the EU demonstrated that some non-EU elites view the EU as a self-interested actor using its economic power to force others to follow its positions (Elgström, 2007; Fioramonti, 2009; Pace, 2009). As a result, non-EU elites have a much more differentiated picture of the EU – with degrees of EU skepticism varying over countries and policies. Especially in regard to economic negotiations and the role of tariffs and subsidies, the EU has been perceived to preaching water while drinking wine (Elgström, 2007; Lucarelli, 2007; but see Scheipers & Sicurelli, 2007 for other negotiations). In contrast, studies on public opinion toward the European Union outside the EU have demonstrated a somewhat more positive attitude among the general public. Citizens around the world show quite favorable feelings toward the EU, with the share of EU friendly attitudes in some regions reaching 80–90% (Schlipphak, 2013a). However, there is one exception to this EU friendly global public opinion.

Recent studies have demonstrated that citizens in Arab countries are much more skeptical toward the European Union than citizens in other countries all over the globe (Isani & Schlipphak, 2017). This is a highly important finding given that the EU – most prominently after the Arab Spring – is strongly interested in influencing domestic developments in the

Arab region. Hence, its non-acceptance among the public endangers its foreign and security policies as well as the success of its developmental policies. That the EU is actually aware of these developments is obvious – not only but most notably in the implementation of the European Neighborhood Barometer (European Commission, 2015).

This book therefore sets out to answer two questions: What factors mainly drive this skepticism in the Arab world? And are the same factors also influencing Muslim citizens' EU attitudes in other parts of the world (making Muslims in general feeling more skeptical toward the EU)?

Some say: it's a cultural thing

As Arab citizens are mostly Muslim and as the finding can be replicated for Arab attitudes toward the UN (Isani, 2018), it might be interpreted as lending credence to the claim of Huntington and others that there is a clash between Islam and the West(ern international organizations) (Huntington, 1993). From this point of view, international cooperation in the form of Western international organizations supposedly following Western norms does not coincide with the Islamic beliefs of Arab citizens, hence leading to strong EU skepticism in this part of the world.

Despite being over 20 years' old, the claim by Huntington and others resonates well with research on the influence of emotional, affective or ideological factors on citizens' attitudes toward the international level. This line of research has focused especially on orientations toward one's nation, toward other countries and groups of citizens and on more general feelings toward global solidarity and openness toward others. Most prominently, Laura McLaren has demonstrated the effect of affective, identity-related perceptions on EU attitudes among the public. First, she argues that one has to differentiate between an inclusive and an exclusive national identity. While the former is defined as a positive pride in one's nation that coincides with the view that others are welcome to share the nation's benefits, the latter is connected to a perception of the world that political psychologists describe as a social dominance orientation. Citizens sharing an exclusive national identity consider their nation and its members to be superior to others and negate the others the right and the ability to become part of their nation. The findings of McLaren demonstrate that it is exclusive feelings that (negatively) influence trust in and perceptions of the European Union and European integration (McLaren, 2002). Furthermore and somewhat based on these thoughts, McLaren later on demonstrated that perceptions of threats from immigration and immigrants – which are closely connected to exclusive nationalist identity feelings – are also strongly influencing citizens' attitudes to the European level. Others have echoed these findings or demonstrated reverse effects, showing that increasing levels of openness (Schoen, 2007) and cosmopolitanism (Ecker-Ehrhardt, 2012) positively influence attitudes toward actors beyond the nation-state. In the past, we have provided a somewhat different point of view that is yet drawn from the angle of identity perspectives (Isani & Schlipphak, 2017). In this article, on which Chapter 1 largely builds upon, we argued that it is the perception of a lack or a future loss of sovereignty that shapes Arab citizens attitudes toward the European Union. While we found empirical evidence for our claim, empirical observations on the aggregate level led us to rethink our theoretical argumentation once again.

Religious Muslims are also usually theorized to view the European Union negatively since they may be against values such democracy and secularism (Pace, 2009). However, in our expectation we are quite skeptical of this logic as we feel that Muslim individual religiosity may have little to do with their attitudes toward the EU.

Others say: it's all about the economy or trust

There are two factors that shed some doubt on this interpretation of Muslim attitudes toward Western institutions in general and the EU more specifically being shaped by affective and value-laden causes. *First*, there obviously is stark difference in the aggregate public EU sympathy between Arab countries. For example, while the EU is viewed quite favorable in Morocco (with about 60% in favor of the EU), citizens are much more skeptical in the neighboring Algeria (20% EU favorable citizens) (Isani & Schlipphak, 2017). In addition, and *second*, further research indicated that citizens in some Muslim-dominated countries in Asia and sub-Saharan Africa demonstrate very positive EU attitudes – 88% EU favorable citizens in the Senegal and over two-thirds of citizens showing EU friendly attitudes in Bangladesh and Indonesia (Schlipphak, 2013b).

These aggregate findings seem to point much more into the direction of a more rational decision making on the side of citizens, highlighting the effect of actual political contexts and events on the one hand and on the use of heuristics on the other. While the former speaks to the validity of long-standing theoretical approaches emphasizing the utilitarian basics of developing attitudes toward the international level, the latter speaks to a line of reasoning that is based on the use of heuristics and that is currently in the process of change. We will add a new nuance to the latter, after outlining first the traditional approaches.

The *utilitarian* approach is – to our knowledge – the chronologically oldest approach to explaining citizens' attitudes toward the international level. In its basic form, it argues that citizens rationally evaluate the costs and benefits associated with an international policy – such as a free trade agreement or a regional integration arrangement. If they come to the conclusion that the policy bears more benefits then costs, they will develop a favorable attitude toward that policy. Research based especially in the US has demonstrated a plentitude of findings that seemingly support this argument – despite the argument's heroic assumption of citizens being informed about the effects of the respective policy. In the European context, researchers have emphasized that citizens perceiving their country's membership in the EU to be favorable toward the country's economic development have a positive attitude toward the EU. This has been called the *sociotropic dimension* of the *utilitarian argument*. That is, citizens are not so much taking their own financial and economic situation or future into account when thinking about international level policies, but consider much more the effects the policy or international cooperation more generally has on the situation of their country and their society. We will come back to this in developing our own argument.

More recently, a new line of research has argued that citizens are not as informed as assumed by the utilitarian approach and thus use *heuristics* or *information shortcuts* when asked about their opinion toward actors and policies on the international level. Probably the first step into that direction was research aiming to identify the extent to which citizens use elite cues to develop their own positions toward the international level. From the viewpoint of that approach, citizens do not hold strong positions about policies beyond the nation-state but rather use the international-level positions of trusted elites as shortcuts. In short: If the domestic actor you believe in is favorable or unfavorable toward the EU, you will simply adopt that position without questioning what the EU does and whether it is of benefit to you or not (De Vries & Edwards, 2009; Steenbergen, Edwards, & De Vries, 2007; Hooghe & Marks, 2005). Yet, the empirical findings on which these theoretical interpretations took place were far from unanimous. Reconsidering similar empirical findings from another point of view, others have argued that the effect of domestic political trust onto trust toward the European level is actually a mechanism they have called transfer of trust. In that understanding, citizens are not informed about their elite positions but simply allocate their high or low levels of domestic political trust to actors on the international level (Harteveld, van der Meer, & De Vries, 2013).

This research resonates well with another strand of research that emphasizes factors which could also be subsumed under the label of heuristics. Johnson demonstrated that citizens' attitudes toward (hegemonic) big states – such as Russia or the US – crucially influence their attitudes toward regional and international organizations of which these states are a member (Johnson, 2011). That is, citizens use cues on the international level that are more accessible – such as the image of a large and rather well-known state – to develop an attitude toward much more unknown and distant international organizations. Similar findings have been demonstrated by Genna (2017) for the EU as well as Steiner (2018) for the case of TTIP – the more one dislikes an important international player (here: a large state) the more one dislikes international cooperation projects of which this player forms a part. While the findings of both of these latter research strands fit well to one another, they have to our knowledge neither been subsumed under a common framework nor been clarified in terms of where these cues come from in the first place. In the remainder, we will outline an argument that includes both of these challenges.

We say: it's about trust gained from political and economic experiences

Heuristics, information shortcuts or cues, are labels for similar if not the same factors influencing public opinion. When an individual confronts a new and unprecedented situation – such as evaluating an object that she or he does not know much about – the individual will search his brain for information that may be used as hints or shortcuts to give a meaningful answer. Such hints can be called heuristics, shortcuts or cues, but they all share the same characteristics: They are easily accessible and easy to process (Kahneman & Tversky, 1972). As such, they are often less complex than the object to be evaluated and they are often the product of long-term socialization processes. An individual's ideological stance – his self-positioning on a political left-right spectrum – is considered to be an important shortcut for the individual when asked to evaluate parties or more specific policies. This shortcut is the product of political socialization – during which the individual reached a self-positioning on the left/right-axis. It is easily accessible because the connotation of politicians and policies as being left or right is often used – and hence salient – in everyday discourse about politics. Heuristics may be employed unconsciously or automatically.

Starting from such an understanding of heuristics, we argue that there are two steps of using heuristics when citizens develop their attitudes toward international actors and policies. *First*, they transfer their attitude toward more well-known domestic or external actors – such as domestic elites or important external states – onto lesser known international actors – such as international organizations.

Second, however, the attitude toward the more well-known external actors is influenced by experiences of the actual current and/or past political and economic behavior of and between the well-known external actor and the home country OR by heuristics that are located within the society and that might be considered an outcome of the above-mentioned interactions. Figure 0.1 demonstrates our two-step model of using heuristics (TSMUH) in developing international level attitudes.

Note that this model includes both the utilitarian and the socio-psychological approach within a coherent argument while at the same time excluding the weaknesses of both approaches. It sheds light on the origin of the attitude toward the more well-known actors which has so far been underexplored in the socio-psychological model of taking cues or heuristics. In addition, it strips the utilitarian model of the heroic assumption that citizens have knowledge of what an IO actually does to evaluate its benefits and costs. Instead, our argument assumes the rational or utilitarian mechanism to set in for the evaluation of actors of which citizens are more aware and more knowledgeable.

To give the reader only one example of why this argument might be highly beneficial to understand and connect previous findings: as outlined earlier, the utilitarian model was one of the first that was used to explain citizen attitudes toward IOs. Yet, its proponents have had a hard time to convince critics that items such as a citizen's satisfaction with the economic situation of his/her home country and its influence should actually be a sign of an utilitarian mechanism that assumes the citizen to actually evaluate the benefits and weaknesses of the IO for the country's economic well-being. Our preceding argument now demonstrates that there might actually be a utilitarian element in the development of attitudes toward the IO. However, the latter is not informed by considering the role of the IO but by considering the role of domestic elites or/and the role of more well-known external actors, like the US, Russia or – within Europe – Germany, the United Kingdom or France. As such, political and economic considerations are a rational element leading to more favorable IO attitudes, but our model

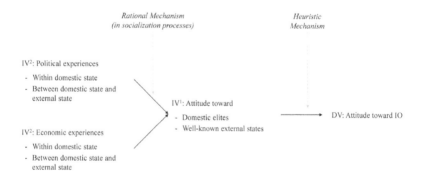

Figure 0.1 The Two-Step Model of Using Heuristics (TSMUH)

argues that the influence of the former is mediated by the attitude toward domestic elites or more well-known external actors.

In addition, our approach now allows for public favorability of or skepticism toward international organizations to greatly vary over countries dependent on the (past) political and economic relations between a country and the (more well-known) member states of that organization. In regard to the European Union, we therefore expect the role of trade, colonial and official development assistance relationships between a respective non-EU country and the EU members to greatly influence, first, citizens' attitudes toward the (important) member states and, second, toward the EU. In the summary of this book's chapters, we will shortly outline the three empirical cases through which we empirically test (parts of) our argument.

In **Chapter 1**, we test our argument using data from the Arab Barometer. Using structural equation modeling, we find that attitudes toward more well-known actors – such as domestic elites and the US – are influencing citizens' attitudes toward the EU as a more distant actor. In addition, these attitudes toward more well-known actors are informed by one's desire for sovereignty. This provides first empirical evidence for our two-step argument.

In **Chapter 2**, we use data from the Afrobarometer together with data on the country level from sources such as the WTO and the OECD. We find that context-level factors – such as the level of trade interdependence between the larger EU countries and the respondent's country, and of the European countries official development assistance toward the respondent's country – substantively influences (Muslim) citizens' attitudes toward the European Union. Leaving aside for the moment the more fine-grained causal mechanism, these findings provide evidence on our expectation that real politics matter.

In **Chapter 3**, we demonstrate that European Muslim citizens are the group most favorable toward the EU compared to all groups of European citizens. We further demonstrate that this favorability is mostly due to European Muslims positive immigration experience, with about 90% of all European Muslims having an immigration background. Being more satisfied with the domestic situation (regarding health, economy, politics) transfers to being more satisfied with the domestic level which then transfers to being more trusting toward the European level. Showing this empirically corroborates the results from the previous chapters and lends even more credence to the empirical substance of our theoretical model.

The **Conclusion** summarizes the findings of the book and gives an outlook on desiderata for future research. Most importantly, we point to the fact that while the data has provided evidence on the usefulness of our theoretical model, the latter actually lacks the component of political communication. We outline how future research should take this component into consideration. In addition, we highlight the relevance and give specific clues for European and domestic policy-making that can be inferred from the findings. However, we also point to the limitations that are still part of this important step to analyzing and understanding external attitudes toward the European Union.

Bibliography

De Vries, C. E., & Edwards, E. (2009). Taking Europe to its extremes. Extremist parties and public Euroscepticism. *Party Politics, 15*(1), 5–28.

Ecker-Ehrhardt, M. (2012). Cosmopolitan politicization? Relating public perceptions of interdependence and expectations in internationalized governance. *European Journal of International Relations, 18*(3), 481–508.

Elgström, O. (2007). Outsiders' perceptions of the European Union in international trade negotiations. *Journal of Common Market Studies, 45*(4), 949–967.

European Commission. (2015). *EU neighbourhood barometer*. Retrieved from www.euneighbours.eu/en/south-east/stay-informed/news/eu-neighbourhood-barometer-2012-2014-opinion-polls-all-available

Fioramonti, L. (2009). *African perceptions of the European Union: Assessing the work of the EU in the field of democracy promotion and peacekeeping*. Retrieved from www.idea.int/sites/default/files/publications/chapters/the-role-of-the-european-union-in-democracy-building/eu-democracy-building-discussion-paper-50.pdf

Genna, G. M. (2017). Images of Europeans: Transnational trust and support for European integration. *Journal of International Relations and Development, 20*(2), 358–380.

Harteveld, E., van der Meer, T., & De Vries, C. E. (2013). In Europe we trust? Exploring three logics of trust in the European Union. *European Union Politics, 14*(4), 542–565.

Hooghe, L., & Marks, G. (2005). Calculation, community and cues: Public opinion on European integration. *European Union Politics, 6*(4), 419–443.

Huntington, S. (1993). The clash of civilizations? *Foreign Affairs, 72*(3), 22–49.

Isani, M. (2018). *Muslim public opinion toward the international order: Support for international and regional actors*. London: Palgrave Macmillan.

Isani, M., & Schlipphak, B. (2017). The desire for sovereignty: An explanation of EU attitudes in the Arab world. *Journal of Common Market Studies, 55*(3), 502–517.

Johnson, T. (2011). Guilt by association: The link between states' influence and the legitimacy of intergovernmental organizations. *Review of International Organizations, 6*(1), 57–84.

Kahneman, D., & Tversky, A. (1972). Subjective probability: A judgment of representativeness. *Cognitive Psychology, 3*(3), 430–454.

Lucarelli, S. (2007). European political identity and others' images of the EU: Reflections on an underexplored relationship. *CFSP Forum, 5*(6), 11–15.

Manners, I. (2002). Normative power Europe: A contradiction in terms? *Journal of Common Market Studies*, *40*(2), 235–258.

McLaren, L. (2002). Public support for the European Union: Cost/benefits analysis or perceived cultural threat? *The Journal of Politics*, *64*(2), 551–566.

Pace, M. (2009). Paradoxes and contradictions in EU democracy promotion in the Mediterranean: The limits of EU normative power. *Democratization*, *16*(1), 39–58.

Scheipers, S., & Sicurelli, D. (2007). Normative power Europe: A credible Utopia? *Journal of Common Market Studies*, *45*(2), 435–457.

Schlipphak, B. (2013a). Actions and attitudes matter: International public opinion towards the European Union. *European Union Politics*, *14*(4), 590–618.

Schlipphak, B. (2013b). Public opinion outside Europe. *LSE EUROPP Blog*. Retrieved from http://blogs.lse.ac.uk/europpblog/2013/06/13/public-opinion-outside-of-europe-is-generally-favourable-toward-the-eu-but-this-is-only-partly-due-to-the-eus-actions/

Schoen, H. (2007). Personality traits and foreign policy attitudes in German public opinion. *Journal of Conflict Resolution*, *51*(3), 408–430.

Steenbergen, M. R., Edwards, E., & De Vries, C. E. (2007). Who's cueing whom? Mass-elite linkages and the future of European integration. *European Union Politics*, *8*(1), 13–35.

Steiner, N. (2018). Attitudes towards the transatlantic trade and investment partnership in the European Union: The treaty partner heuristic and issue attention. *European Union Politics*, *19*(2), 255–277.

1 Arab citizens' attitudes toward the European Union

When sovereignty is the c(l)ue[1]

Introduction

As already outlined in the introduction of this book, there is one significant exception to the EU's positive image around the world. Arab citizens are much more skeptical toward the EU – as well as toward other international organizations such as the United Nations (UN) or the International Monetary Fund (IMF) – than citizens in other world regions. Despite the EU's long-standing interest in the democratization and stabilization of the Middle East, no analytical research has so far been undertaken to explain this Arab skepticism toward the EU.

Based on literature on anti-Americanism as well as on EU public opinion in general, we argue that Arab citizens' views on international organizations – of which the EU is but one prominent example – and their policies are dependent on three factors: the desire for sovereignty that has its origins in citizens' political and cultural experience within their domestic setting, the degree of trust in domestic actors, and citizens' attitudes toward the US, the latter being an effect of the US policies in the Middle East. Testing these arguments with Arab Barometer (AB) data,[2] we demonstrate that all of these indicators influence Arab citizens' perceptions of the EU. It is, however, the cue of sovereignty that matters most. We discuss this finding and its consequences, along with remaining methodological and empirical desiderata, at the end of the chapter.

What influences Arab attitudes toward the EU?
Expectations combining our argument with
earlier findings from the literature

There currently exists a large body of literature on European citizens' attitudes toward the EU, its institutions and European regional integration,

as well as on attitudes among citizens of the Global North toward international organizations and international ideas – such as free trade – in
general (see, among many others, Harteveld, van der Meer, & De Vries,
2013; Boomgaarden, Schuck, Elenbaas, & de Vreese, 2011; Mansfield &
Mutz, 2009; Scheve & Slaughter, 2001). Yet, only since the mid-2000s has
research turned to the views of elites and citizens in Asia, Latin America
and sub-Saharan Africa toward these institutions. Using elite interviews,
Chaban, Elgström, Kelly, and Yi (2013) show that EU perceptions vary
regionally and according to issue area. For example, the EU is seen positively as a trading partner among elites interviewed in Africa, Southeast
Asia and the Pacific. However, internal divisions within the EU are viewed
negatively in Africa and Southeast Asia. Lucarelli (2014) summarizes the
qualitative research on the external image of EU mostly based on elite
interviews. She concludes that knowledge of the EU is relatively low,
especially in the developing world, and that the EU is mostly viewed as an
economic power.

While some studies have looked into the feelings of citizens about regional
integration in Africa, East Asia, Southeast Asia and Latin America (Jhee,
2009), others have turned to global or regional public opinion vis-à-vis
international organizations such as the UN (Dellmuth & Tallberg, 2015;
Johnson, 2011), international financial institutions (Edwards, 2009) or the
EU (Chaban, Elgström, Kelly, & Yi, 2013; Chaban & Holland, 2014; Schlipphak, 2013; Lucarelli, 2007; Chaban, Elgström, & Holland, 2006). In general, previous research has found the theoretical approaches and empirical
findings derived from the American or European contexts to be more or less
generalizable to other locations across the globe. Economic satisfaction or
positive financial perceptions ('utilitarianism') and citizens' trust in domestic actors ('elite cues') correlate positively with favorable attitudes toward
the international arena, as do higher education levels, and a general openness toward others and external actors ('cosmopolitanism,' Ecker-Ehrhardt,
2012). Interestingly, the attitudes toward international actors demonstrated
by citizens in the Global South are – despite these citizens' lack of knowledge about what these actors actually do – on average much more favorable
than they are in the Global North (Schlipphak, 2013).

There is, however, one notable exception to this trend: in most of the
Arab countries between 20% and 40% of citizens express favorable attitudes toward international organizations.[3] Despite the increasing role that
the Arab region has played (and continues to play) in recent international
politics, this puzzle of unfavorable Arab public opinion has not yet really
been tackled by scholars. Although area studies experts like Shibley Telhami (1993, 2013), Anour Boukhars (2011) and Mohamed Zayani (2008)

all point toward the crucial role of public opinion for elite decision making, even in the strictly authoritarian systems of the Levant, only a few analytical approaches have been undertaken thus far to explain the international attitudes of Arab citizens.

To come to theoretical expectations regarding Arab citizens' attitudes toward the EU, we have to first combine previous research on Arab public opinion and on global attitudes toward International Organizations (IOs) – especially the EU. We base our argumentation on our main two-step argument but also refer back to the three broad lines of analysis that exist for citizens' international attitudes (see, for example, Hooghe & Marks, 2005), focusing on how they are apt for our argument.

The two-step argument

In our main argument, we presented a two-step scenario according to which the experiences of citizens with their domestic elites and external states translate into more specific and well-developed attitudes toward these elites and are then shaping attitudes toward more distant international players, such as the EU. In the remainder, we will use the literature on anti-Americanism, post-colonialism and the Arab Spring to demonstrate that previous experiences have shaped citizens' attitudes toward *sovereignty*, their *domestic elites* and the *US* which then again translates into their feelings toward the European Union.

First step: behavior of domestic and external actors, sovereignty considerations and negative feelings toward domestic elites and well-known external actors

In contrast to literature arguing that Arab citizens' attitudes toward society and politics, as well as Western values, are strongly shaped by their religion (Islam) and Arab heritage (Al-Kandari & Gaither, 2011), more elaborate research has turned to the relevance, origins and effects of sovereignty considerations among the Arab public. Hashemi argues that the origins of the Arab Spring are lying in two levels of dignity: an individual one and a collective one. Whereas the individual level of dignity relates to personal perceptions about the well-being of individuals, "the theme of 'Arab indignity' also exists on a collective level, and it is associated with a set of common historical experiences, which partly explains why it is such a potent force in the politics of the region" (Hashemi, 2013, p. 209f). According to Hashemi's interpretation, the desire for sovereignty – as a sub-dimension of collective dignity – results from European colonialism and the (perceived)

Western support for authoritarian rulers in the region after the Second World War. Reviewing recent books on the current situation in the Arab region, he notes that the question of becoming (collectively) sovereign – understood as being generally independent from external rule – lies at the core of the Arab Spring movements. To make his point, he cites a Syrian human rights activist according to whom we "need a second independence in Syria. The first was from the French and the second will be from the Assad dynasty" (Hashemi, 2013, p. 210). Hashemi goes on by stating that "[t]hese sentiments are widely felt and apply to Zine El Abidine Ben Ali in Tunisia, Muammar Qaddafi in Libya, Hosni Mubarak in Egypt, and beyond" (Hashemi, 2013, p. 210).

This view has been echoed by other authors, stating that "the uprisings in each country have been distinct in their motivations; however, among the common denominators has been a sense that people are calling for greater dignity (karame) in standing up to their regimes" (Hermez, 2011, p. 527f). (See also on this point Paust, 2013; Glasius & Pleyers, 2013). El Bernoussi (2015) – after discussing different understandings of dignity in greater length – argues that the two events of the 1956 nationalization of the Suez Canal and the Arab Spring events specifically taking place in Egypt can be seen as

> a recurring call for dignity by the Egyptian people. This call unveiled the important nature of the call for dignity that stemmed from a social malaise and linked to economic and political disempowerment and oppression. These needs [. . .] refer to a particular postcolonial context. This context emerged from the European colonial experience that saw the expression of a native nationalism as a quest for the Self at the level of a nation.
>
> (El Bernoussi, 2015, p. 379)

Based on this literature, we argue that the broader concept of dignity is mirrored in its core values of sovereignty and self-determination (Hashemi, 2013; Telhami, 2013). They are stimulated and corroborated by the meddling of more well-known external actors (such as the US or France) in domestic politics or by the negligence of Arab sensitivities by Western actors (Lynch, 2003), leading citizens to react negatively to any actor perceived to exert such outside interference or inattention (Telhami, 2013; Boukhars, 2011).

The point of Arab attitudes to be influenced by the actual behavior of (well-known) external actors has also been substantiated by research on Arab citizens' Anti-Americanism. Furia and Lucas (2006, 2008) found that a pan-Arabic identity and respective framing endeavors by domestic elites mainly influence Arab citizens' international attitudes. They argue that the (perceived) behavior of an external state toward any Arab country crucially shapes citizens' attitudes in all Arab states toward that specific external state (Furia & Lucas, 2006). They attribute their finding to the seemingly strong regional identity shared throughout the Arab region, which forms the baseline against which a given external actor's actions are evaluated. Using a Zogby dataset, Furia and Lucas (2008) are able to show that the salience of the Palestine crisis not only strongly influences Arab citizens' attitudes toward the US, but also toward Canada, France, Germany and the United Kingdom.

Summing up this paragraph, we argue that Arab sovereignty considerations are caused by the behavior of domestic as well as (well-known) external actors. Second, following the literature, we expect these sovereignty concerns to (negatively) influence the attitudes of Arab citizens toward the respective actors, the domestic elites and the US. Third, we argue that these sovereignty concerns should also shape Arab citizens' EU attitudes. But how exactly should this work out?

Second step: how sovereignty feelings translate to EU attitudes

In this section, we argue that sovereignty concerns – caused by the actual behavior of states and elites – influence EU attitudes via the mediating variables of citizens' attitudes toward the actors causing the sovereignty concerns. That is, we argue that sovereignty concerns lead in a first step toward more negative feelings toward domestic elites and external actors. Second, we argue that these negative feelings are then used as cues/heuristics to evaluate a more distant and less-known international organization such as the EU. While we introduced the first part of this argument in the previous section, the latter part of the argument – using attitudes toward more well-known actors as cues – has already found some evidence in the literature. We outline this second step using evidence from previous findings in the remainder.

Some years ago, Johnson (2011) has shown that citizens' attitudes toward a state that is perceived to crucially influence a particular IO actually also shapes citizens' feelings toward that IO as well. Descriptive research has demonstrated that Western organizations in general are perceived by Arab citizens as being under American rule (WPO, 2008). Utilitarian considerations of Arab citizens regarding the costs and benefits which they associate with the US should, hence, bring them to reflect their stance toward the EU. Therefore, we also expect that negative feelings toward the US – whose behavior in the Middle East should be much more familiar to Arab citizens

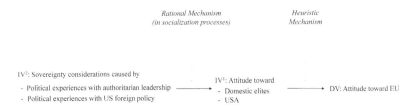

Figure 1.1 Explaining EU attitudes among Arab citizens: the two-step model

than the EU's actions are (Chiozza, 2007, 2009) – have a detrimental effect on Arab citizens' EU attitudes.

Furthermore, research on public opinion about the EU, toward regional and international organizations, as well as on Arab anti-Americanism has pointed toward the significant influence thereon of citizens' trust in domestic elites. Within most of the previous studies of which we are aware, governmental trust/satisfaction is positively correlated to citizens' attitudes toward both the US and toward IOs. A more recent and convincing approach explains this finding by arguing that citizens are not so much taking informed cues but rather transferring their trust in domestic actors and governmental parties onto the international level – that is, trusting the domestic governments translates to trusting the EU or the UN (see, e.g., Dellmuth & Tallberg, 2015; Harteveld et al., 2013). Conversely, not trusting one's domestic elites should result in not trusting more distant international organizations. For the Arab world, we expect citizens' lower trust in their domestic government to result in lower EU favorability. Figure 1.1 summarizes all of our expectations visually.

Data and analysis

The data for our analysis comes from the Arab Barometer's third wave. The AB is a widely used dataset for analyzing Arab attitudes on freedom, democracy and religion, as well as domestic and international actors. In the third wave the survey was held in Jordan, Palestine, Lebanon, Egypt, Sudan, Algeria, Morocco, Yemen, Kuwait, Libya, Tunisia and Iraq.[4] The total number of respondents in the 12 countries surveyed was 14,809, of which 87.7% of the original sample expressed an opinion about the EU. In what follows, we will concentrate on this third wave (fielded in 2013 and 2014) while also presenting results from the former second wave (fielded in 2010 and 2011) to take the potential effects of the Arab Spring into account.

By comparing the findings for time points during early Arab Spring and after these events, we are able to demonstrate whether different factors on the individual level matter differently at different points in time. To mirror our theoretical argument empirically, we employ structural equation modeling. We set up a model in which citizens' attitudes toward the EU are a function of citizens' levels of anti-Americanism and trust in domestic political actors. Both concepts were again estimated as functions of citizens' sovereignty feelings. Furthermore, we included control variables that directly affect EU attitudes.

Our main dependent variable is a respondent's favorability toward the EU. Unfortunately, the AB does not ask this question directly so we use a proxy question asking where the influence of the EU in the promotion of democracy in the country lies between very positive (coded as 5) to very negative (coded as 1). A very positive view of the EU is taken to be indicative of very high EU favorability whereas a very negative view of the EU is taken to be demonstrative of very low EU favorability.[5] For the aggregate measure, we separate all citizens demonstrating very favorable or favorable attitudes toward the EU (coded as 1) from all other citizens (coded as 0).

To measure a citizen's *desire for sovereignty*, the variable 'external demands for reform' is used as a proxy – coded as 4 when the respondent felt that the external demand for reform was acceptable and as 1 when it was seen as unacceptable due to its harming of their country's own national interests. We operationalized *US favorability* by the respondent's view about Americans: 1 is coded for strong agreement that Americans are good people and 0 for disagreement that Americans are good people. Finally, citizens' trust in domestic political actors is captured by the variable 'Government satisfaction.' This variable measures citizen's trust in governmental elites, and is coded on a 0–10 scale of satisfaction.

Furthermore, we control for six additional variables. The first three of these variables consist in the usual socio-demographic controls – education, age and gender. 'Higher education' – assumed to positively influence citizens' attitudes toward external actors – is coded 1 if a respondent had a post-secondary level education and 0 if otherwise. 'Female' is coded 0 if male and 1 if female. 'Age' is the reported age of the respondent measured in years, where the minimum age for taking the questionnaire is 18 years old.

Second, we control for citizens' levels of religiosity and their closeness to religious actors/elites. Religiosity and closeness to religious actors are included as Blaydes and Linzer (2012) have demonstrated that not only piety (strong religiosity) but also the closeness to Islamist groups significantly influences US attitudes of Muslim citizens. Hence, one should control for the effects of these variables on citizens' attitudes toward other Western actors. We measure 'religiosity' through an individual's self-perception of his/her own degree of religiosity.[6] The question used to code this variable asks whether one sees oneself as religious, where 1 corresponds to not religious, 2 to somewhat religious, and 3 to religious. One's closeness toward religious groups is measured by a variable asking citizens for the extent to which the respondent agreed that religious leaders should have an influence over government decisions: 4 corresponds to strong agreement and 1 corresponds to strong disagreement, with values 2 and 3 measuring attitudes laying between these poles. Finally, we control for citizens' country of origin, using dummy variables for each country (except Jordan, being the reference category).

Findings

Table 1.1 shows the descriptive statistics for both the dependent and independent variables. For the dependent variable, when measured on a 5-point scale the aggregate mean of Arab public opinion vis-à-vis the EU seems

Table 1.1 Descriptive statistics

Variables	Mean	Min-Max	N	Std. Dev.
Dependent Variable				
EU Favorability	3.0	1–5	12,986	1.2
Independent Variables				
Ideational Mechanism				
(*H1*) Openness Preference	2.5	1–3	14,167	0.7
(*H2*) External Demands	2.2	1–4	13,685	1.0
Utilitarian Mechanism				
(*H3*)Economic Future	3.2	1–5	14,213	1.3
(*H4*) US Favorability	0.58	0–1	12,179	0.5
Cue-Taking Mechanism				
(*H5*) Government Satisfaction	3.9	0–10	14,282	3.0
Controls				
Religiosity	2.3	1–3	14,417	0.6
Trust in Religious Leaders	2.2	1–4	13,807	0.9
Higher Education	0.28	0–1	14,776	0.45
Female	0.5	0–1	14,809	0.5
Age	37.8	18–89	14,799	13.9

Source: Arab Barometer Third Wave (2012–14).

actually neutral. Yet, when calculating EU favorability separately for each of the countries, the mean values vary to some degree. In fact, Algerian citizens are most critical of the EU (Mean = 2.4) while Moroccans are demonstrating the most favorable EU feelings (Mean = 3.6). These differences across countries show the empirical need to control for a citizen's origin in the structural equation model.

Regarding the independent variables, Arab citizens are quite skeptical regarding externally requested reforms. This mirrors a refusal to being lectured by international actors on what to do domestically and also lends some first credence on our expectations regarding citizens' desire for sovereignty. Regarding their feelings toward the US – which are measured by citizens' perception of US American citizens – Arab citizens are on average seeing Americans as good people. Finally, Arab citizens' satisfaction with their own government is low. Country-specific means rang from a low of 1.8 (in Lebanon) to a high of 6.4 (in Kuwait) which indicates that there is a (unsurprising) connection between governmental satisfaction and economic outlooks, at least on the aggregate level.

Coming to the controls, Arab citizens perceive themselves as being highly religious. Yet, they are somewhat feeling distant toward religious actors. The descriptive statistics further show that the data sample is well-balanced in terms of gender, educational attainment and the age groups of participants.

We then employed the structural equation model explained previously. Table 1.2 and Figure 1.2 plot the findings of the SEM based on a Gaussian identity linkage function. Generally speaking, the independent variables of the first (anti-Americanism and trust in domestic actors) and of the second order (sovereignty concerns) behave as expected in explaining variation in the dependent variable. The variable 'external demand for reforms' which measures our causally prior conceptual indicator – citizens' desire for sovereignty – turns out to be substantially and significantly influencing citizens' anti-Americanism but not citizens' trust in domestic actors. That is, sovereignty concerns might only be relevant in influencing external attitudes. This, however, might also be due to the variable used to measure sovereignty that explicitly refers to external interventions. Regarding the direct explanation of EU attitudes, the two mediating variables – anti-Americanism and trust in domestic actors – both significantly and substantially explain variation in the dependent variable. Again, however, the effect of anti-Americanism seems to be somewhat stronger even taking the different scaling of both variables into account. As the SEM reports standardized coefficients, the effect of Anti-Americanism seems ten times as strong as the effect of trust in domestic actors.

Table 1.2 Explaining EU attitudes among Arab citizens

	EU Favorability
US Favorability	0.36*** (0.02)
Government Satisfaction	0.04*** (0.00)
Religiosity	−0.06***(0.02)
Trust in Religious Leaders	0.01 (0.01)
Higher Education	−0.06* (0.03)
Female	−0.01 (0.02)
Age	−0.00** (0.00)
	US Favorability
External Demands	0.09***(0.00)
	Government Satisfaction
External Demands	0.01 (0.02)
N	13,585

Source: Arab Barometer Third Wave (2012–14). Own calculations. Structural equation model (SEM) with country fixed effects (not plotted); Standard errors in parentheses. * = significant at the 0.05 level; ** = significant at the 0.01 level; *** = significant at the 0.001 level.

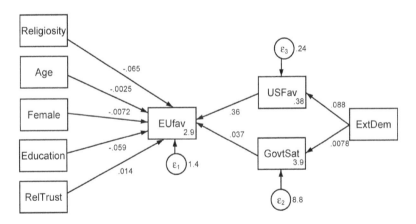

Figure 1.2 Visualization of the SEM results

Regarding the controls, higher levels of religiosity and age seem to negatively influence EU feelings. In contrast, one's closeness to religious actors, education and gender have no significant effects on EU favorability.

Furthermore, the findings demonstrate that the country origin of respondents has in part strong effects on citizens' EU attitudes. Coming from

Algeria, Egypt, Iraq, Tunisia, Lebanon and Sudan substantially and significantly decreases one's level of EU sympathy (on average), while coming from Kuwait, Libya, Morocco and Yemen significantly and substantially increases EU favorability among citizens. On first sight, this country effect does not follow an obvious pattern (such as countries in which uprisings found (no) EU support during the Arab Spring, or countries with more European tourists being more EU friendly). Hence, these findings only show that factors on the country level – such as previous experiences with external actors – greatly matter for citizens' attitudes. Future studies will have to discover which external factors – and their communication by domestic elites – turn out to be of explanatory power.

Robustness checks

To lend more credence to the reliability and validity of our findings, we first check for differences between the third wave of the Arab Barometer – our main dataset – and the second wave, which was fielded in 2010 and 2011.[7] For the country cases included in both waves, aggregate EU favorability did not change much over the years (except for Lebanon and Tunisia). Second, we also check for multicollinearity between the independent variables by using a Spearman rank correlation matrix. This shows that none of the correlations between the independent variables are a cause for concern. Third, we re-estimate the structural equation model using an (ordinal) logit linkage function for estimating EU favorability. The direction and significance of the independent variables remain the same. Overall, the empirical explanation is robust across time and across different methods of estimation and model conceptualizations.

Discussion and conclusion

We started from the observation that Arab public opinion toward the EU – and other Western actors – is generally quite skeptical, and in contrast to global public opinion. Using the main two-step argument of this book, we argued in this chapter that sovereignty considerations – that are an effect of political experiences with (authoritarian) domestic political actors and with more well-known external actors such as the US – are influencing EU attitudes but are mediated by more specific attitudes toward these more well-known actors.

Testing these expectations with AB data demonstrated that our expectations can be cautiously confirmed. Citizens who perceive external demands for reform as harmful to their own national interests – which we considered a valid proxy for their desire for sovereignty – demonstrate a significantly and substantially higher probability of having unfavorable feelings toward the US (but not toward their domestic actors). Furthermore, our findings demonstrate that it especially is this attitude toward the US that substantially and significantly shapes EU attitudes – to a much stronger degree than the (significant) factor of domestic political trust or citizens' degree of religiosity.

Summing up these findings of a first empirical step to explain Arab citizens' comparably negative EU attitudes, therefore, we might attribute this specific negativity in the Arab region to two fundamental points. First, the action and politics of the US – but also of the EU in attempting to gain more and more influence outside their borders – might be seen especially critical in this part of the world given that the desire for sovereignty is quite important in Arab political discourse. Second, one of the factors seen as most strongly influencing international attitudes – trust in or satisfaction with *domestic* political actors – is quite negative in the Arab world. Hence, the domestic context matters as well. Combining both interpretations of these findings, Arab citizens do not trust their domestic actors as much as citizens in other parts of the world *and* do not trust the most powerful actors in global politics as well. The really bad news for the EU is that Arab citizens do not consider the EU as a neutral organization to which to turn to as a consequence of disliking domestic and US actors. Instead, the EU seems to be perceived as being another instrument or partner of already disliked institutions.

An implication of this finding is that the EU should work with local stakeholders in various Middle Eastern countries so as not to give the impression that its policies in the regions are trying to impose something from the outside. Additionally, in working with local stakeholders and representatives of non-EU countries in general, the EU should obviously do a much better job in acting as partners instead of trying to push agendas in a way which have often been perceived as a top-down-process (see Elgström, 2007; Scheipers & Sicurelli, 2007, 2008; Emerson & Young, 2007; Pace, 2009). In this way, the EU might be able to disconnect itself from other (and more disliked) actors – a first step to gaining more public sympathy in the future.

Coming to further findings of our studies, religiosity and the role of religious elites – which we included as control variables – seem to be less important than was originally assumed in the literature. The effect of citizens' closeness toward religious actors is not significant, despite earlier empirical findings regarding the significant effects of religious framing (Blaydes & Linzer, 2012) and the influence that area study experts accredit to Muslim religious leaders (Al-Kandari & Gaither, 2011). Second, the significant effect of citizens' religiosity is actually limited in size. Hence, we do not consider the effect of religiosity to be a strong predictor of EU attitudes. Therefore, and this might come as a surprise to some proponents of values being the most important factor influencing Arab public opinion toward the West, religious feelings do not seem to play that big a role in explaining Arab citizens' attitudes toward the EU.

Nonetheless, dealing with such an underexplored topic always comes with certain caveats. Our preliminary conclusions come with methodological caveats which we have already discussed. The most important one might be that we were not able to compare our findings based on the AB with other datasets. While the Pew Global Attitudes Survey offers data on the EU favorability of citizens of some Arab countries over the last 15 years, it (somewhat erratically) stopped asking citizens for their levels of elite trust after 2007. In contrast, the European Neighborhood Barometer asks these questions but only began its measurement of these after 2012, and – maybe even more astonishingly – does not include questions on citizens' levels of religiosity. Hence, we were able to somewhat control for the descriptive similarity of aggregate EU skepticism in the respective Arab countries between different data sources. The findings of PEW and AB data demonstrates that the level of EU skepticism in the countries included in both surveys is comparable. In addition, there seems to be no fundamental trend in a more positive or more negative direction of Arab EU attitudes. Rather, these attitudes seem – again, in the aggregate and maybe not on the individual level – to be quite stable over time. Still, our findings presented in this article are mostly dependent on one single data source.

Theoretically, we have aimed to include individual level factors that literature on public opinion toward the EU has already discussed. Yet, we have done so introducing a new argument and somewhat brushing against the lines of some former theoretical argumentation. Still, we consider the two-step causal argument of the book here to be more coherent and empirically stronger than previous research discussing multiple factors influencing EU attitudes at the same time. Second, what we have not fully captured by focusing on individual-level effects on the subject of Arab citizens' EU attitudes is the theoretical explanation of the context effects that we found by introducing country dummies in our structural equation model. As our findings suggest, there seems to be variance among Arab countries in favorability of the EU that we only to a very limited degree have confronted so far. These differences on the aggregate level between countries point toward effects of historical and real-politics context in the relationship between a respective country, the EU and some of the former colonial powers among the EU's member states. While we used country dummies in the empirical models to empirically control for these differences, taking them into theoretical account in future explorations of the subject will lead us toward a more comprehensive understanding of the sources of Arab citizens' EU skepticism.

Despite these remaining problems, by introducing a two-step flow argument on the desire for sovereignty related to broader concept of Arab dignity and its (potential) role in determining citizens' EU attitudes through the mediation variable of anti-Americanism, our research has shed some first light on why Arab citizens' view the EU much more unfavorably than citizens in other parts of the world. As our empirical findings are not only statistically significant but also substantively relevant, and as our robustness checks lend further credence to our theoretical claims, we are confident that we have presented a robust general picture of upon what further research and political behavior can and should be based. In the two chapters following, we will not only analyze EU attitudes from Muslim citizens in other parts of the world but also delve much deeper into the role of context factors influencing these attitudes.

Notes

1 This chapter is an adapted version of our article in *Journal Common Market Studies* on "The Desire for Sovereignty: An Explanation of EU Attitudes in the Arab World" (Isani & Schlipphak, 2017). The authors are grateful to John Wiley and Sons for allowing us the secondary use of that article under License Number: 4280810892841 (License Date: February 2nd, 2018). We encourage our readers to also have a look at the original paper that is accessible via DOI: 10.1111/jcms.12485.

2 We use the AB instead of sources such as the Pew Global Attitudes Survey or the European Neighborhood Barometer, as the AB provides data for a greater number of countries and a wider variety of indicators. A full discussion of data choice can be found in the methodology section.

3 When EU favorability is coded as a binary variable, the countries of the Arab world are seen to have a generally negative opinion of the EU. The two countries in the Maghreb that defy this trend are Morocco and Libya, with 59% (Morocco) and 58% (Libya) of respondents demonstrating favorable EU attitudes respectively.

4 These are the countries covered by this wave of the Arab Barometer. The sample thus excludes Bahrain, Saudi-Arabia, Qatar and others. Still, the Arab Barometer provides the most comprehensive and most qualitative dataset for measuring attitudes of Arab citizens and seems hence to be the best dataset available for this first analysis of Arab citizens' EU attitudes.

5 To check the validity of our proxy we turn to the Pew Global Attitudes surveys conducted during the same time periods that directly pose the question of EU favorability. The comparison of the results shows similar trends in citizens' feelings toward the EU. Comparing especially the aggregate percentages of citizens clearly liking the EU demonstrates that our DV in the AB actually measures respondents' EU favorability. Unfortunately, we could not use the Pew Global

Attitudes dataset as a second (robust) source for our main analysis because many of the questions that help in coding for our independent variables were not part of these survey years.

6 Praying daily or on Fridays, which may be used as another measure of religiosity, is known to overestimate the degree of religiosity in majority Muslim countries as compared to other countries. For example, in the third wave of the AB around 78% of respondents reported attending Friday prayers but only 38% of them saw themselves as religious.

7 In the first wave, no indicator on EU favorability was included.

Bibliography

Al-Kandari, A., & Gaither, T. K. (2011). Arabs, the west and public relations: A critical/cultural study of Arab cultural values. *Public Relations Review*, *37*(3), 266–273.

Blaydes, L., & Linzer, D. A. (2012). Elite competition, religiosity, and anti-Americanism in the islamic world. *American Political Science Review*, *106*(2), 225–243.

Boomgaarden, H. G., Schuck, A. R. T., Elenbaas, M., & de Vreese, C. H. (2011). Mapping EU attitudes: Conceptual and empirical dimensions of Euroscepticism and EU support. *European Union Politics*, *12*(2), 241–266.

Boukhars, A. (2011). The Arab revolutions for dignity. *American Foreign Policy Interests*, *33*(2), 61–68.

Chaban, N., Elgström, O., & Holland, M. (2006). The European Union as others see it. *European Foreign Affairs Review*, *11*(1), 245–262.

Chaban, N., Elgström, O., Kelly, S., & Yi, L. S. (2013). Images of the EU beyond its borders: Issue-specific and regional perceptions of European Union power and leadership. *Journal of Common Market Studies*, *51*(3), 433–451.

Chaban, N., & Holland, M. (2014). *Communicating Europe in times of crisis: External perceptions of the European Union*. London: Palgrave Macmillan.

Chiozza, G. (2007). Disaggregating anti-Americanism: An analysis of individual attitudes towards the United States. In P. Katzenstein (Ed.), *Anti-Americanisms in world politics* (pp. 93–128). Ithaca, NY: Cornell University Press.

Chiozza, G. (2009). A crisis like no other? Anti-Americanisms at the time of the Iraq War. *European Journal of International Relations*, *15*(2), 257–289.

Dellmuth, L., & Tallberg, J. (2015). The social legitimacy of international organisations: Interest representation, institutional performance, and confidence extrapolation in the United Nations. *Review of International Studies*, *41*(3), 451–475.

Ecker-Ehrhardt, M. (2012). Cosmopolitan politicization? Relating public perceptions of interdependence and expectations in internationalized governance. *European Journal of International Relations*, *18*(3), 481–508.

Edwards, M. S. (2009). Public support for the international economic organizations: Evidence from developing countries. *Review of International Organizations*, *4*(2), 185–209.

El Bernoussi, Z. (2015). The postcolonial politics of dignity: From the 1956 Suez nationalization to the 2011 revolution in Egypt. *International Sociology*, *30*(4), 367–382.

Elgström, O. (2007). Outsiders' perceptions of the European Union in international trade negotiations. *Journal of Common Market Studies*, *45*(4), 949–967.

Emerson, M., & Young, R. (2007). Political Islam and the European neighbourhood policy. In M. Emerson & R. Young (Eds.), *Political Islam and European foreign policy* (pp. 1–11). Brussels: CEPS Paperback Series.

Furia, P. A., & Lucas, R. (2006). Determinants of Arab public opinion on foreign relations. *International Studies Quarterly*, *50*(3), 585–605.

Furia, P. A., & Lucas, R. (2008). Arab Muslim attitudes toward the west. Cultural, social and political explanations. *International Interactions*, *34*(1), 186–207.

Glasius, M., & Pleyers, G. (2013). The global moment of 2011: Democracy, social justice and dignity. *Development & Change*, *44*(3), 547–567.

Harteveld, E., van der Meer, T., & De Vries, C. E. (2013). In Europe we trust? Exploring three logics of trust in the European Union. *European Union Politics*, *14*(4), 542–565.

Hashemi, N. (2013). The Arab spring two years on: Reflections on dignity, democracy, and devotion. *Ethics & International Affairs*, *27*(2), 207–221.

Hermez, S. (2011). On dignity and clientelism: Lebanon in the context of the 2011 Arab revolutions. *Studies in Ethnicity and Nationalism*, *11*(3), 527–537.

Hooghe, L., & Marks, G. (2005). Calculation, community and cues: Public opinion on European integration. *European Union Politics*, *6*(4), 419–443.

Isani, M., & Schlipphak, B. (2017). The desire for sovereignty: An explanation of EU attitudes in the Arab world. *Journal of Common Market Studies*, *55*(3), 502–517.

Jhee, B. K. (2009). Public support for regional integration in Northeast Asia: An empirical test of affective and utilitarian models. *International Political Science Review*, *30*(1), 49–65.

Johnson, T. (2011). Guilt by association: The link between states' influence and the legitimacy of intergovernmental organizations. *Review of International Organizations*, *6*(1), 57–84.

Lucarelli, S. (2007). European political identity and others' images of the EU: Reflections on an underexplored relationship. *CFSP Forum*, *5*(6), 11–15.

Lucarelli, S. (2014). Seen from the outside: The state of the art on the external image of the EU. *Journal of European Integration*, *36*(1), 1–16.

Lynch, M. (2003). Taking Arabs seriously. *Foreign Affairs*, *82*(5), 81–94.

Mansfield, E. D., & Mutz, D. C. (2009). Support for free trade: Self-interest, sociotropic politics, and outgroup anxiety. *International Organization*, *63*(3), 425–457.

Pace, M. (2009). Paradoxes and contradictions in EU democracy promotion in the Mediterranean: The limits of EU normative power. *Democratization*, *16*(1), 39–58.

Paust, J. J. (2013). International law, dignity, democracy, and the Arab Spring. *Cornell International Law Journal*, *46*(2), 1–19.

Scheipers, S., & Sicurelli, D. (2007). Normative power Europe: A credible Utopia? *Journal of Common Market Studies*, *45*(2), 435–457.

Scheipers, S., & Sicurelli, D. (2008). Empowering Africa: Normative power in EU-Africa relations. *Journal of European Public Policy*, *15*(4), 607–623.

Scheve, K., & Slaughter, M. J. (2001). What determines individual trade-policy preferences? *Journal of International Economics*, *54*(2), 267–292.

Schlipphak, B. (2013). Actions and attitudes matter: International public opinion towards the European Union. *European Union Politics, 14*(4), 590–618.

Telhami, S. (1993). Arab public opinion and the Gulf War. *Political Science Quarterly, 108*(3), 437–452.

Telhami, S. (2013). *The world through Arab eyes.* New York: Basic Books.

World Public Opinion (WPO). (2008). *People in Muslim nations conflicted about UN.* Retrieved from http://worldpublicopinion.net/people-in-muslim-nations-conflicted-about-un/

Zayani, M. (2008). Courting and containing the Arab street: Arab public opinion, the Middle East and US public diplomacy. *Arab Studies Quarterly, 30*(2), 45–64.

2 Actual behavior matters

The EU's external policies and Muslim EU attitudes across regions[1]

Introduction

In the previous chapter, we identified the desire for sovereignty – mediated by trust in domestic actors and anti-Americanism – to strongly influence Muslim citizens' EU attitudes at least in the Arab world. We argued that the desire for sovereignty and the consequential attitudes toward domestic and external actors is based on citizens' actual experiences with the political actions of external actors. But is that really convincing given what we know about the (lack of) citizens' interest in and knowledge of (international) politics?

In this chapter, we turn toward this exact question, leaving aside for a moment the two-step explanatory mechanism we identified in the introduction and successfully tested in Chapter 1. Here, we concentrate on the effects of actual experiences with the EU on EU attitudes, somewhat neglecting the causal mechanism leading from these experiences (via trust in domestic and external actors) to EU attitudes.

What context factors may explain citizens' attitudes toward external actors? Previous descriptive research has already ascribed elite as well as public feelings to the EU to the EU's international behavior, focusing especially on the EU's role in economic negotiations and cooperation (Chaban & Holland, 2008; NCRE, 2007; Elgström, 2007; Lucarelli, 2007). We argue here that economic interactions – predominantly in the form of trade interactions and the flow of official development assistance (ODA) from Europe to a citizen's country – should indeed explain Muslim citizens' attitudes toward the EU. However, we also highlight that from a more cultural perspective it may also be experiences related to a country's identity and past that still influence public EU perceptions. In this regard, we argue that a common colonial past of a country and a member of the EU as well as the form of the ending of that past (be that peaceful or violent) should have important implications for a country's citizen's EU sympathy.

We test both parts of the argument using the PEW Global Attitudes Survey dataset, supplemented by several contextual indicators. The empirical findings demonstrate that the EU's actions via official developmental assistance (ODA) and with regard to trade relations have a substantial and significant effect on Muslim citizens' attitudes across regions, while the colonial past between a country and EU member states did not matter.

These findings have two important implications. First, for researchers analyzing the effects of public attitudes on governmental preferences (see, e.g., Finke, 2009; Koenig-Archibugi, 2004; Burstein, 2003), these results indicate that public opinion toward the EU and toward international institutions in general is actually influenced – at least in the first step – by contextual factors. Second, the results indicate that non-EU citizens also form their feelings toward international organizations by evaluating the actual behavior of the organization. We will return to these thoughts in the final chapter of the book. This finding appears especially noteworthy for researchers and practitioners focusing on the role of the EU as a norm-diffusing actor in international relations. They should be interested in the fact that the EU's external behavior actually appears to matter – at least with regard to its image worldwide. However, this news comes as a finding with contrary implications. Whilst the effect of the EU's spending on ODA might positively influence its future image, the effect of the EU's trade relationships with other countries might be counterproductive in the EU's attempt to position itself as a normatively good and, therefore, legitimate global leading power.

Feelings toward the EU

Actual behavior matters – expectations at the contextual level

The EU has long promoted and simultaneously demanded the implementation of democratic and humanitarian norms (for recent analyses, see Levitz & Pop-Eleches, 2010; Freyburg, Lavenex, Schimmelfennig, Skripka, & Wetzel, 2009; Fioramonti, 2009; Pace, 2009) as well as the deepening of regional integration projects beyond its own borders (De Lombaerde & Schulz, 2009; Hettne & Söderbaum, 2005). In general, researchers agree that the EU must be credible and trustworthy to promote its ideas and to be perceived as a leading power (and, therefore, as a role model). However, such a positive perception of the EU is not universally held. Scheipers and Sicurelli have demonstrated that the EU has been regarded as inconsistent in negotiations over the Kyoto protocol as well as in the implementation of the International Criminal Court. This inconsistency, they argue, has led political elites outside Europe to perceive the EU as a not always trustworthy actor (Scheipers & Sicurelli, 2007). This perception appears to be especially applicable for political elites from sub-Saharan Africa (Scheipers & Sicurelli, 2008). Elgström (2007) and Chaban, Elgström and Holland (2006) point out that political elites across the globe consider the EU a trading power. However, actors participating in bargaining within the WTO do not conceive the EU to be a leading power. Rather, political actors across the globe are disappointed that the EU strongly urges other countries to open their borders and to abolish tariffs to promote free trade while remaining highly protectionist in regard to European (agrarian) interests (Lucarelli, 2007). Such a lack of consistency has also been considered a serious problem for the establishment of an effective role for the EU in the democratization of the Mediterranean region (Pace, 2009, p. 49). As one of the few authors addressing this issue, Pace emphasizes the high relevance of public opinion for the credibility and, thus, effectiveness of European foreign policy activities. Otherwise, Pace argues, the dissemination of ideas by the EU might again be perceived as a neo-colonial effort to globally promote European or Western values such as liberal democracy (Pace, 2009, p. 50f).

There are only two studies that use systematic approaches[2] to analyzing perceptions of the EU beyond the European Union: Lucarelli's "The External Image of the EU" (Lucarelli, 2007) and the NCRE project initiated by Chaban and Holland. The latter has demonstrated that political elites throughout the Asian-Pacific and sub-Saharan regions overwhelmingly share negative perceptions of the EU. Whilst the EU has been regarded as a successful model of regional economic integration, several criticisms have been lodged against its foreign policy (NCRE, 2007, see for its many results: Chaban & Holland, 2014). The uncritical fashion in which the EU interacts with the People's Republic of China particularly worries Asian elites. Additionally, in a conclusion of their project, Chaban and Holland state that the EU is perceived as "1) an actor whose policy is severely influenced by its own security concerns, [as] 2) a neo-liberal actor in its attitude to the abroad, [and as] 3) a protectionist power" (NCRE, 2007, Section 12; also: Lucarelli, 2007). Similarly, political elites in sub-Saharan Africa are worried by the European Union's motives and development strategies, perceiving it to be bureaucratic and protectionist (NCRE, 2007, Section 10; also: Fioramonti, 2009). Following a similar argument, Hettne and Söderbaum speak of the EU practicing a form of soft imperialism in areas of inter-regional cooperation. Fioramonti (2009) and Söderbaum (2007) also emphasize that the EU's approach of strongly connecting developmental aid and economic cooperation to political conditionality is perceived as a forcible dissemination of Western ideas. Both authors argue that such ideas are often perceived as conflicting with a recently resurgent sense of an autonomous and independent African political and cultural tradition.

All of these findings appear to indicate that the image of the EU is strongly connected to its actions, especially in the areas of international economic negotiations and cooperation. Thus, we should expect outcomes, politics and policies to strongly shape public opinion toward the EU.[3] The literature has demonstrated that elite opinion toward the EU is mainly dependent on the EU's behavior in international economic negotiations and cooperation; hence, citizens' positions should also be shaped by the effects of trade and financial cooperation with the EU (for a similar argument on EU citizens, see Jones & van der Bijl, 2004). These effects should have a positive influence on the non-EU elites' as well as the citizens' feelings toward the EU if cooperation in trade and finance with the EU is beneficial to the elites' and citizens' country.

In addition, the official development assistance (ODA) provided by the EU and its member states may affect citizens in their everyday lives. In contrast to most other policies, ODA has been connected to cooperation with local civil societies, and thus, the ODA activities of the EU (or its larger member states) might strongly influence citizens' feelings. Especially in very poor and developing countries, the EU (and/or its member states) might be seen as an actor that generously supports the development of these countries by lending technical as well as financial support.

Somewhat in contrast, other research – mostly on the EU positions of elites – has indicated that that the EU's tendency to grant economic cooperation and financial support only in combination with political coercion is perceived critically, especially in countries which experienced more problematic colonial pasts with member states of the EU (see also McCann, 2003). That is, the EU's combination of economic and moral policies should be met with greater resistance in countries that have been under colonial rule from current EU member states – most importantly, the United Kingdom, France, the Netherlands, Spain, Portugal and Germany. The reasoning behind this argues from a more historical-ideational perspective. Citizens should be more skeptical toward an intervention into domestic politics when this intervention is coming from a country that is thought of as having harmed a citizen's country *in the past*, by not allowing independence. Hence, the difference between the first and the second line of argument is one between policies (economic vs. moral) and between time points (current vs. historical). In the line with our main argument outlined in the introduction that highlights a more rational explanatory mechanism of EU attitudes among Muslim citizens, we argue that the former should have a stronger effect than the latter.

In conclusion, the expectations on the context level can be summarized as follows.

H1a: A non-EU citizen in a country with a higher benefit from trade with the European Union should be more likely to have a favorable feeling toward the EU.

H1b: A non-EU citizen in a country with a higher dependency on European development assistance should be more likely to have a favorable feeling toward the EU.

H2: A non-EU citizen in a country with a more recent colonial relationship with EU member states and that experienced conflict over the ending of that colonial relationship should be less likely to have a favorable feeling toward the EU.

H3: The economic factors outlined in H1a and H1b should have a stronger explanatory power than the moral factors outlined in H2.

Methodology

Data

The basic dataset used in this paper is the PEW Global Attitudes Survey conducted in 2007 (PEW, 2007), which includes 47 countries. The number of respondents varies between 500 (Ukraine) and 3,142 (China). As we are only interested in the case of Muslim attitudes (see Schlipphak, 2013 for more comprehensive research on external EU attitudes), we restrict ourselves to study only citizens which identify themselves as Muslim. Our overall data is composed of 12,261 Muslim respondents in 28 countries[4] outside the EU. The PEW data have rarely been used within the scientific community beyond research on anti-Americanism (e.g., Chiozza, 2009; Furia & Lucas, 2008; but see also Shu & Nakamura, 2010; Kleinberg & Fordham, 2010). While less is known about the strengths and weaknesses of these data compared with other surveys (Norris, 2008; Heath, Fisher, & Smith, 2005), this dataset provides remarkable advantages that largely outweigh the potential problems associated with the lack of study it has received.[5] This survey not only measures public opinion toward the European Union within all the countries included but also offers indicators – such as the attitude toward free trade and feelings toward other international organizations (IOs) – that cannot be found in other datasets. Finally, and in contrast to datasets such as the Gallup Survey "Voice of the People 2007" (Gallup Foundation, 2007) or the Bertelsmann Foundation survey on "World Powers of the 21st century" (Bertelsmann Foundation, 2006), the PEW dataset provides most of the indicators usually considered necessary to explain political attitudes in general (that is, indicators of political trust as well as socio-demographic indicators). Still, all of the findings will be interpreted cautiously, as it is always appropriate for survey data, especially for data from less-developed contexts (see Seligson, 2005).

Operationalization

The *dependent variable* (eu_eval) was calculated by measuring respondents' favorable and unfavorable feelings toward the EU. The rank order of the original variable was reversed, now ranging from 1 (very unfavorable) to 4 (very favorable). Only including respondents in the calculation who have an opinion toward the EU reduces the number of cases to 9,635 (approximately 83.3% of the original number of cases). While the mean of non-responding citizens per country is 16.7%, there is variance between the countries, ranging from 3.7% of missing values in Jordan to 44.6% in Pakistan. This variance in citizens' knowledge of the EU among countries might cause measurement problems. As clarified below, we address these differences by integrating a control variable at the contextual level.

As the data are situated at two levels and as we wish to demonstrate the effects of both contextual- and individual-level factors, a multilevel model appears appropriate. A calculation of the unconditional intra-class correlation with

$$\frac{\upsilon}{\upsilon + \pi^2 / 3}$$

where υ represents the random-intercept variance (see Rabe-Hesketh & Skrondal, 2008, p. 304), yields a value of the intra-class correlation of 0.11. This result indicates that 11% of the total variance and, therefore, a non-negligible amount of variance exists *between* countries (the second level of analysis). Hence, a multilevel regression method will be applied.

The independent variable for *H1a* was calculated as

$$trade\ surplus = \frac{e - i}{gdp}$$

where e is the amount of a country's exports to the EU (in US Dollars in 2007, based on data from the International Monetary Fund [IMF, 2018]), i is the amount of a country's imports from the EU (in US Dollars in 2007, data from the IMF [IMF, 2018]), and gdp is a country's total Gross Domestic

Product (GDP, in US Dollars in 2007, adjusted for Purchasing Power Parity, data from the World Bank [World Bank, 2018]).

The independent variable for *H1b* was operationalized as the share of the EU's ODA to a country in relation to its total GDP (ODA provided by all European countries, by the European Commission and by the Council of Europe in 2007, data from the OECD [OECD, 2018]).

H2 was more difficult to operationalize because nearly all of the countries surveyed have a colonial past with one of the EU member states. The argument here is that direct remembrance of colonialism must be vivid for it to have a significant effect on respondents' attitudes. Citizens who have experienced a colonial past themselves should still represent a significant part of the population. Hence, we consider it reasonable to attribute the term 'recent colonial past' to all countries that became independent after 1946 (that is, 60 years prior to the year of the survey, 2007). Therefore, the dummy variable capturing the recent colonial past separates countries that have become independent in the last 60 years (= 1) from all other countries (= 0). Because *H2* expects an interaction between the recent colonial past and a problematic, i.e., violent, end to colonialism, we additionally coded a dummy variable separating countries that became sovereign following a violent (= 1) or peaceful (= 0) process. The coding was based on data from the CIA World Factbook (CIA, 2012) and the Library of Congress Country Studies (Library of Congress, 2012) as well as countries' official websites. Countries with the value '1' in an interaction of these two colonial variables have a recent and violent colonial past with EU member states. Non-EU citizens within these countries should be more likely to be skeptical toward the EU.

On the individual level, we controlled for several factors potentially influencing citizens' attitudes. From the perspective of researchers pointing to the effect of utilitarian considerations, a citizen's attitude toward free trade might strongly influence one's feeling toward the European Union. Hence, we included a variable asking for the respondent's attitude toward free trade (with values from 1 = very bad to 4 = very good). Second, research on the utilitarian mechanism has also indicated that citizen's levels of education might play a role. Hence, we calculated two dummy variables containing information on the formal education status of the respondents (Lower Education = no or primary education, Higher Education = at least some form of tertiary education). Including two dummy variables instead of one ordinal education variable is necessary given that the ordinal ranking of school education is not exactly comparable across the countries surveyed.

From a more ideational perspective and following again on the traces of Huntington's argument (Huntington, 1993), the level of religiosity might play a role for Muslim citizens' attitudes toward the EU. For example, in studies of EU attitudes of deeply religious Muslim elites, the openness of the way of life within the EU is a point of criticism (Emerson & Young, 2007; but see also Furia & Lucas, 2008). Additionally, even within the EU, deeply religious respondents have displayed skepticism toward the EU's liberal 'way of life' (Jasiewicz, 2004; but also Boomgaarden & Freire, 2009). Hence, we added an ordinal variable labeled 'religiosity' (from 1 = not religious at all to 4 = very religious) to the equation.

Finally, we additionally control for four important societal measures. First, on the context level, the degree of aggregate EU knowledge might play a role. We might expect that in countries with greater knowledge of the EU, respondents are more likely to have direct contact with the EU. However, one could either expect that respondents with closer contact with the EU know more about the positive life circumstances within the EU (which could result in a positive effect of greater knowledge of the EU) or know more about the EU's 'iron curtains' when it comes to securing its borders (which may result in a negative effect of greater knowledge). In any case, we control for such possible effects of an uneven distribution of EU knowledge over countries by including a control variable on the contextual level by measuring the percentage of citizens per country with knowledge of the EU (that is, the percentage of citizens able to express a feeling regarding the EU). Second, on the individual level, we control for societal trust, gender and age. Generalized or societal trust was measured by a question asking respondents whether most people in their society are trustworthy. Again, the rank order of the original variable was reversed, now ranging from 1 (strongly disagree) to 4 (strongly agree). Having more generalized trust might also transfer into a more positive feeling toward external actors. In addition, being older might be connected to having a greater closed-mindedness and therefore to a more negative feeling toward the EU, while women (especially in some of the developing countries studied here) might be more distant from political life overall and more skeptical toward unknown foreign political actors. Therefore, a gender dummy variable and an ordinal variable measuring the age of respondents (four values, ranging from 1 = 18–30 years to 4 = above 60 years) were added to the equation. All the variables used within the explanatory models are described by common univariate statistics in the web appendix.

Explaining non-EU citizens' feelings toward the EU

Empirical results

To test both parts of the argument, we ran three multilevel regression models with an ordinal logistic link function. All of the independent and control variables are treated as fixed effects, whilst only the intercept is included as random. The first model only includes the contextual variables, whilst the second model by contrast exclusively focuses on the independent variables on the individual level. In the third model, all variables (including the control variables on the contextual and the individual levels) are taken into account. Table 2.1 presents the results of these calculations.

In the contextual model both the ratio of exports to imports from the EU as well as dependency on ODA from the EU are significant and positive in affecting favorability of the EU. However, colonial rule and its ending are not significant in affecting feelings toward the EU. This shows initial support for *H1a*, *H1b*, *H3*, however not for *H2*.

Table 2.1 Explaining Muslim EU attitudes across regions

	Contextual Model	Individual Model	Full Model
(*H1a*) Ratio Exports to/Imports from EU	0.103***		0.119***
	(0.032)		(0.027)
(*H1b*) Dependency on ODA from EU	0.640***		0.651***
	(0.126)		(0.076)
(*H2*) Colonial Rule	−0.082		0.076
	(0.375)		(0.283)
(*H2*) Problematic Ending	0.192		0.228
	(0.223)		(0.148)
EU Knowledge			1.699*
			(0.692)
Attitude toward Free Trade		0.247***	0.263***
		(0.068)	(0.070)
Lower Education		−0.202**	−0.151*
		(0.065)	(0.076)
Higher Education		0.030	0.027
		(0.073)	(0.076)
General Trust		0.115*	0.115*
		(0.053)	(0.52)
Religiosity			−0.207**
			(0.075)
Gender			0.004
			(0.055)
Age			−0.079*
			(0.039)
Log Likelihood	−9,611.796	−9,067.904	−9,011.051
Number of Cases	8,004/22	7,596/22	7,568/22

Sources: PEW Global Attitudes Survey 2007/OECD/IMF/WB. Own calculations. Standard errors in parentheses. Weighted by Design Weight. *** = significant at the .001 level; ** = significant at the .01 level; * = significant at the .05 level.

The individual attitudes toward free as well general trust are significant and positive in affecting feelings toward the EU. These results are consistent with the previous literature and theory as those who are more open to free trade are more likely to be open toward international actors. Second, as argued in the other chapters people are likely to transfer their trust on the societal level to that on the international level so the positive affect of social trust on feelings toward the EU does not come as a surprise. While higher education is insignificant in affecting feelings toward the EU, low or no education is significantly and negatively affecting feelings toward the EU. Again the latter result is consistent with expectations as those with a lower education are likely to be less open toward outside actors (see especially Hainmueller & Hiscox, 2007).

The full model reinforces support for *H1a*, *H1b*, *H3* but not for *H2*, in which appropriate control variables are included in the model. The hypotheses that a beneficial relationship with the EU in terms of trade and developmental assistance will be transferred into positive feeling toward the EU is bolstered as shown by the continuing positive and significant relationship. Since the effect of colonialism remains insignificant and the effect of economics is positive and significant, there is further support for *H3*. Interestingly, a couple of control variables show significant and negative effects toward EU favorability. Those that are older in age are more likely to be negative toward the EU as would be expected by a predictably more conservative older population. Also, those more religious are also less likely to have positive feelings toward the EU. Although in the other chapters of the book religiosity is mostly insignificant in predicting EU attitudes, here it shows a significantly negative relationship. This may also be a function of the PEW sample which consists of Muslims from both Muslim majority as well non-Muslim majority countries. Finally, the control variable for EU knowledge also depicts significantly positive effects of feelings toward the EU which we would expect of individuals that have a greater interest in the EU.

Robustness checks

To check whether the results presented are not artifacts of model selection or choice of dependent variable, we recalculated the full model with a multilevel logit model using a binary dependent variable (with the respondent being favorable coded as 1, otherwise 0). In addition, we also ran a single-level heteroskedastic ordered logistic model. In the single-level model, standard errors were clustered around countries. Both models demonstrate similar effects to those found in the multilevel analysis with an ordinal dependent variable.

Conclusion

This chapter set out to test one of the main assumptions behind our theoretical model that we outlined in the introduction – can we really expect context factors resulting from a country's interaction with a distant international actor to influence citizens' attitudes toward that distant actor?

Briefly summarizing the results of a multilevel model as well as robustness checks, the analysis supports our argument. Besides the substantial effect of citizens' attitudes toward free trade as a proxy for their general position toward international and supranational cooperation, contextual-level variables also matter. A country's dependence on ODA distributed by the EU or its member countries as well as trade with the EU significantly influences the probability of respondents being more favorable toward the EU. Yet, a country's historical past with the EU – that is, a context factor mirroring a more ideational or historical factor – did not play a role in influencing Muslim citizens' attitudes. This further confirms our expectation that the reasons underlying Muslims' EU attitudes are at least as rational or utilitarian as for citizens of other denominations.

Furthermore, the chapter offers two important insights for connected literature but also points to an important research desideratum that we tackle in more detail in the concluding chapter. Regarding the implications, authors focusing on the legitimacy of IOs as such (see again Dellmuth & Tallberg, 2015; Ecker-Ehrhardt, 2011; Spilker, Schaffer, & Bernauer, 2012; also Keohane, 2011; Zürn, 2004) should be interested in the fact that feelings toward different IOs can be explained by similar independent variables. Thus, perceptions of an IO's legitimacy might be improved (or worsened) by the IO's behavior, but they are also dependent on citizens' individual attitudes.

Second, based on the interpretation of contextual-level effects as elite-induced effects, authors who are more interested in the EU's self-conception as a wielder of 'soft power' or 'normative power' (Nye, 2004; also see Manners, 2002; Aggestam, 2008; critically: Hyde-Price, 2006) might be puzzled by these results. The EU is widely perceived in a favorable light by citizens across the globe. Normatively, this may contribute to a relatively high degree of acceptance of the EU and its actions. Such acceptance is necessary for an actor aiming to diffuse norms, including actions that interfere in domestic behavior to promote norms and values of good governance. However, the consequences of the effects of the actual trade relationship on citizens' feeling toward the EU might worry researchers and practitioners from a normative standpoint. The EU trade relationship with a specific country has an impact on respondents' feelings toward the EU. Assuming that the general direction of the effects is correctly captured by these findings, it seems reasonable to state that if the country exports more to the EU than it imports, its citizens are more likely to feel favorable toward the European organization. Inversely, the findings also indicate that the more negative a country's trade relationship, the more likely the respondents are to feel unfavorably toward the EU. This finding appears even more important because most of the countries *import* much more *from* the EU than they *export to* it. That is, the trade effect in most of the countries may make citizens more skeptical toward the EU. Under the assumption that the EU does not wish to alter this situation, its current attempts to improve its ability to diffuse norms and values by obtaining a more prominent profile in world politics might be counterproductive. An increase in the EU's public profile (especially in countries with a trade deficit with the EU) may increase global skepticism toward the EU.

The research desideratum coming with these findings focuses on how these context factors actually affect individual-level attitudes of citizens. While we demonstrated the effects, we are up to now unsure how they happened. Most probably, a crucial part of the explanation concerns the role of (domestic) elite communication about and positions toward the European Union. Yet, a different explanation that is more closely in line with our theoretical model would argue that it is the effect of the interactions between a citizen's country and the EU on citizens living conditions that affect citizen's attitudes – not only toward their domestic actors, but also toward more distant actors. We will outline such an argument for the case of Muslim citizens in the EU in Chapter 3.

Notes

1   This chapter is a strongly adapted version of Bernd Schlipphak's earlier article in *European Union Politics:* Schlipphak, B. (2013). Actions and Attitudes matter: International Public Opinion towards the European Union. *European Union Politics*, *14*(4), 590–618. Copyright © 2013 (Bernd Schlipphak). Reprinted by permission of SAGE Publications. The authors are grateful to SAGE publishing for allowing us the secondary use of that article. We encourage our readers to also have a look at the original paper that is accessible via DOI: 10.1177/1465116513482527.

2   Furthermore, an empirical study of perceptions of the EU was performed amongst Chinese scholars and university students (Liqun, 2008). However, its main finding was that both Chinese scholars and students are very fond of the constructive role of the European Union but that this fondness may be biased by some "sort of wishful thinking" (Liqun, 2008, p. 169). Additional studies have addressed or at least provided indicators of interest for research on citizens' views of the EU beyond European borders. However, these data usually lack indicators regarding the general political attitudes of the respondents and sometimes fail to provide socio-demographic indicators of the respondents by which to explain these attitudes. Such is the case for the Bertelsmann Foundation's

research on World Powers in the 21st century (Bertelsmann Foundation, 2006) and Gallup International's Voice of the People survey in 2007 (Gallup Foundation, 2007). Therefore, to our knowledge, no analytical study has been undertaken of the sources of EU support outside European borders based on the data from these studies.

3 That is not necessarily to say that citizens have actual knowledge of the EU and, therefore, evaluate it in relation to its actual behavior. The argument we developed in the very first chapter states that the actual (ODA and trade) policies of the EU might – by influencing the country's economy or welfare system – shape citizens' attitudes toward domestic actors and then translate into trust toward the EU (for more on the argument of cue-taking, see Anderson, 1998; Steenbergen, Edwards, & De Vries, 2007; Gabel & Scheve, 2007).

4 The countries included are Bangladesh, Ethiopia, Ghana, India, Indonesia, Israel, Ivory Coast, Jordan, Kenya, Kuwait, Lebanon, Malaysia, Mali, Nigeria, Pakistan, Russia, Senegal, South Africa, Tanzania, Turkey, Uganda and Ukraine. In addition to the EU countries, the test excluded China, Morocco, Egypt and the Palestinian territories due to missing data on the contextual or individual level. Finally, we had to drop the US and Canada due to another missing data problem. Checks revealed that there are actually no observations in these countries containing answers to all questions measuring the independent variables on the individual level. This is due to the fact that the questionnaire was split in two divergent forms in both countries, ascribing different questions of the survey to different parts of the sample.

5 However, the methodological information given by the PEW Global Attitudes Project for every survey is very informative in this regard. There are differences in modes of surveying (face-to-face via telephone) and sampling design as well as problems with the oversampling of urban areas in some countries. Unfortunately, these problems are common in most cross-regional survey research (especially in research outside Europe).

References

Aggestam, L. (2008). Introduction: Ethical power Europe? *International Affairs*, *84*(1), 1–11.

Anderson, C. J. (1998). When in doubt, use proxies. Attitudes toward domestic politics and support for European integration. *Comparative Political Studies*, *31*(5), 569–601.

Bertelsmann Foundation. (2006). *World powers in the 21st century*. Retrieved from www.cap.lmu.de/download/2006/2006_GPC_Survey_Results.pdf

Boomgaarden, H. G., & Freire, A. (2009). Religion and euroscepticism: Direct, indirect or no effect? *West European Politics*, *32*(6), 1240–1265.

Burstein, P. (2003). The impact of public opinion on public policy. *Political Research Quarterly*, *56*(1), 29–40.

Central Intelligence Agency (CIA). (2012). *The world factbook*. Retrieved from www.cia.gov/library/publications/the-world-factbook/

Chaban, N., Elgström, O., & Holland, M. (2006). The European Union as others see it. *European Foreign Affairs Review*, *11*(1), 254–262.

Chaban, N., & Holland, M. (Eds.) (2008). *The European Union and the Asia-Pacific: Media, public, and elite perceptions of the EU.* London: Routledge.

Chaban, N., & Holland, M. (2014). *Communicating Europe in times of crisis: External perceptions of the European Union.* London: Palgrave Macmillan.

Chiozza, G. (2009). A crisis like no others? Anti-Americanism at the time of the Iraq War. *European Journal of International Relations, 15*(2), 257–289.

De Lombaerde, P., & Schulz, M. (Eds.) (2009). *The EU and world regionalism. The makability of regions in the 21st century.* Cornwall: Ashgate.

Dellmuth, L., & Tallberg, J. (2015). The social legitimacy of international organisations: Interest representation, institutional performance, and confidence extrapolation in the United Nations. *Review of International Studies, 41*(3), 451–475.

Ecker-Ehrhardt, M. (2011). Cosmopolitan politicization: How perceptions of independence foster expectations in international institutions. *European Journal of International Relations, 18*(3), 481–508.

Elgström, O. (2007). Outsiders' perceptions of the European Union in international trade negotiations. *Journal of Common Market Studies, 45*(4), 949–967.

Emerson, M., & Young, R. (2007). Political Islam and the European neighbourhood policy. In M. Emerson & R. Young (Eds.), *Political Islam and European foreign policy* (pp. 1–11). Brussels: CEPS Paperback Series.

Finke, D. (2009). Domestic politics and European treaty reform: Understanding the dynamics of governmental position-taking. *European Union Politics, 10*(4), 482–506.

Fioramonti, L. (2009). *African perceptions of the European Union: Assessing the work of the EU in the field of democracy promotion and peacekeeping.* Retrieved from www.idea.int/sites/default/files/publications/chapters/the-role-of-the-european-union-in-democracy-building/eu-democracy-building-discussion-paper-50.pdf

Freyburg, T., Lavenex, S., Schimmelfennig, F., Skripka, T., & Wetzel, A. (2009). EU promotion of democratic governance in the neighbourhood. *Journal of European Public Policy, 16*(6), 916–934.

Furia, P. A., & Lucas, R. E. (2008). Arab Muslim attitudes toward the west: Cultural, social, and political explanations. *International Interactions, 34*(2), 186–207.

Gabel, M., & Scheve, K. (2007). Mixed messages. Party dissent and public opinion on European integration. *European Union Politics, 8*(1), 37–59.

Gallup Foundation. (2007). *Voice of the people survey 2007.* Retrieved from www.icpsr.umich.edu/icpsrweb/ICPSR/studies/21441

Hainmueller, J., & Hiscox, M. J. (2007). Educated preferences: Explaining attitudes toward immigration in Europe. *International Organization, 61*(2), 399–442.

Heath, A., Fisher, S., & Smith, S. (2005). The globalisation of public opinion research (CREST Working Paper 109/2005).

Hettne, B., & Söderbaum, F. (2005). Civilian power or soft imperialism? The EU as a global actor and the role of interregionalism. *European Foreign Affairs Review, 10*(4), 535–552.

Huntington, S. (1993). The clash of civilizations? *Foreign Affairs, 72*(3), 22–49.

Hyde-Price, A. (2006). 'Normative' power Europe. A realist critique. *Journal of European Public Policy, 13*(2), 217–234.

International Monetary Fund (IMF). (2018). *Direction of trade statistics*. Retrieved from www.imf.org/en/data

Jasiewicz, K. (2004). Knocking on Europe's door: Voting behavior in the EU accession referendum in Poland. *Problems of Post-Communism, 51*(5), 34–44.

Jones, E., & van der Bijl, N. (2004). Public opinion and enlargement. A gravity approach. *European Union Politics, 5*(3), 331–351.

Keohane, R. O. (2011). Global governance and legitimacy. *Review of Political Economy, 18*(1), 99–109.

Kleinberg, K., & Fordham, B. O. (2010). Trade and foreign policy attitudes. *Journal of Conflict Resolution, 54*(5), 687–714.

Koenig-Archibugi, M. (2004). Explaining government preferences for institutional change in EU foreign and security policy. *International Organization, 58*(1), 137–174.

Levitz, P., & Pop-Eleches, G. (2010). Why no backsliding? The European Union's impact on democracy and governance before and after accession. *Comparative Political Studies, 43*(4), 457–485.

Library of Congress. (2012). *Country studies*. Retrieved from http://lcweb2.loc.gov/frd/cs/profiles.html

Liqun, Z. (2008). Chinese perceptions of the EU and the China-Europe relationship. In D. Shambaugh, E. Sandschneider, & Z. Hong (Eds.), *China-Europe relations. Perceptions, policies and prospects* (pp. 148–173). London/New York: Routledge.

Lucarelli, S. (2007). European political identity and others' images of the EU: Reflections on an underexplored relationship. *CFSP Forum, 5*(6), 11–15.

Manners, I. (2002). Normative power Europe: A contradiction in terms? *Journal of Common Market Studies, 40*(2), 235–258.

McCann, G. (2003). Recolonisation by stealth: Global market liberalisation and the EU's development policy. *Journal of Contemporary European Studies, 11*(2), 215–229.

National Centre for Research on Europe (NCRE). (2007). External perceptions on the EU. Presentation of results, Brussels.

Norris, P. (2008). The globalization of comparative public opinion research. In N. Robinson & T. Landman (Eds.), *The SAGE handbook of comparative politics* (pp. 522–540). London: Sage.

Nye, J. S. (2004). *Soft power: The means to success in world politics*. New York: PublicAffairs.

Organisation for Economic Co-operation and Development (OECD). (2018). *Data on the official development assistance*. Retrieved from https://data.oecd.org/oda/net-oda.htm#indicator-chart

Pace, P. (2009). Paradoxes and contradictions in EU democracy promotion in the mediterranean: The limits of EU normative power. *Democratization, 16*(1), 39–58.

PEW. (2007). *Spring 2007 global survey data*. Retrieved from www.pewglobal.org/dataset/spring-2007-survey-data/

Rabe-Hesketh, S., & Skrondal, A. (2008). *Multilevel and longitudinal modeling using stata* (2nd ed.). College Station, TX: Stata Press.

Scheipers, S., & Sicurelli, D. (2007). Normative power Europe: A credible Utopia? *Journal of Common Market Studies*, *45*(2), 435–457.

Scheipers, S., & Sicurelli, D. (2008). Empowering Africa: Normative power in EU-Africa relations. *Journal of European Public Policy*, *15*(4), 607–623.

Schlipphak, B. (2013). Actions and attitudes matter: International public opinion towards the European Union. *European Union Politics*, *14*(4), 590–618.

Seligson, M. A. (2005). Improving the quality of survey research in democratizing countries. *PS: Political Science and Politics*, *38*(1), 51–56.

Shu, M., & Nakamura, H. (2010). Public perceptions and regional cooperation in East Asia. *WLAS Research Bulletin*, *2*.

Söderbaum, F. (2007). African regionalism and EU-African interregionalism. In M. Telo (Ed.), *European Union and new regionalism* (pp. 185–221). Cornwall: Ashgate.

Spilker, G., Schaffer, L., & Bernauer, T. (2012). Does social capital increase public support for economic globalization? *European Journal of Political Research*, *51*(6), 756–784.

Steenbergen, M. R., Edwards, E. E., & De Vries, C. E. (2007). Who's cueing whom? Mass-elite linkages and the future of European integration. *European Union Politics*, *8*(1), 13–35.

World Bank. (2018). *Data on national gross domestic product*. Retrieved from http://data.worldbank.org/

Zürn, M. (2004). Global governance and legitimacy problems. *Government and Opposition*, *39*(2), 260–287.

3 From everyday experience to EU attitudes

The case of European Muslim citizens[1]

Introduction

As we outlined in the introductory chapter, Arab countries – and particularly their Muslim residents – are among the most skeptical of the European Union (EU) and other international institutions (Schlipphak, 2013). This seems to resonate with claims that immigrants, particularly Muslim immigrants, threaten European identity, freedoms, culture and political stability (Andrews, 2009; Cantle, 2001; Sarrazin, 2010). Other research indicates that anti-Muslim perceptions among the European public lead to more negative perceptions toward the European Union and European policies (e.g., Azrout & Wojcieszak, 2017; Erisen & Kentmen-Cin, 2017). At the core of such debates often lies the question of whether there is something particular about Muslims or the religion of Islam that makes Muslims incompatible with European values and therefore the European political system (Diamond, Plattner, & Brumberg, 2003; Esposito & Voll, 1996; Huntington, 1993; Ross, 2001).

So far, we have argued that Muslim citizens are actually highly rational in developing their attitudes toward the European Union. We drafted a causal model that puts forward a two-step model of explaining (Muslim) citizens' attitudes toward the EU, demonstrating that actual political experiences with domestic or external actors lead to a (consistent) attitude toward these actors that is then transferred to more distant and unknown actors such as the European Union. In the first chapter, we demonstrated that this model finds empirical evidence for Arab citizens, with our model only being able to fully capture the second step of the model. In the second chapter, we additionally showed that the political behavior of the EU also substantially influences EU attitudes, leaving however the actual explanatory mechanism aside for the moment. In this third chapter, we now turn to a full test of our explanatory model by asking two, so far neglected, questions: How favorably do European Muslim residents perceive the European Union? And, why do they hold these attitudes toward the EU?

The two-step argument which we are testing in this chapter is based on our conceptualization in the introduction but additionally fed by current American politics literature on immigrant political trust. In the two-step model, we argue that citizens – when asked to evaluate international actors – use the shortcut of trust in domestic or more well-known external actors. They simply transfer or extrapolate their feelings toward more well-known domestic actors to the less-known actors at the international level (Armingeon & Ceka, 2014; Harteveld, van der Meer, & De Vries, 2013). This is the second step of our model. For the first step, leading from actual experiences to these attitudes toward more well-known actors, mostly US-based research has shown that trust in domestic actors is based on immigrants' satisfaction with the situation in their host country compared to their country of origin (Alba & Nee, 2003; Dancygier & Saunders, 2006; de la Garza, Falcon, & Garcia, 1996; Maxwell, 2010a, 2010b, 2013; Röder & Mühlau, 2011, 2012; Waters, 1999). Given that an overwhelming majority of Muslim residents in the EU have an immigrant background, we develop an argument that slightly deviates from the transfer of *trust* logic outlined earlier but still falls within the theoretical framework of our conceptualization. We argue that European Muslims base their trust in domestic and European actors on their degree of satisfaction with their domestic situations. That is, we expect a transfer of *satisfaction* logic to be at work for European Muslims, with the latter extrapolating the satisfaction with their domestic political and economic systems onto the European level. The consequence of this theoretical elaboration is that we assume Muslims to be more favorable toward the EU (and domestic actors) than other groups.

We test our expectations with data from the European Social Survey (ESS) waves from 2002 to 2014, and find empirical support for our theoretical argument: Muslims are more trustworthy of their domestic political actors and of the EU compared to any other (non-)religious group. Also, satisfaction with their political, health and economic situation strongly informs their trust in domestic as well as in European actors, hence confirming both steps of our argument. This has major implications. Even though Muslims in Europe may come from a different cultural background or may be more fundamentalist than their non-Muslim counterparts (Koopmans, 2015), this does not appear to translate into political distrust of the EU (see, also, Erisen, 2017). In fact, one might actually argue that these higher levels of trust are even a positive sign of political integration and engagement (Morales & Giugni, 2011).

European Muslims and domestic trust

How do European Muslims feel about the EU and why? In what follows we argue that European Muslims should be more favorably disposed toward their domestic political institutions and toward European institutions. To build the argument, we first outline why European Muslims, who mostly have a migrant background, should develop a favorable attitude toward their domestic institutions – the first step of our model. Next, we elaborate on the transfer of satisfaction logic which should translate this domestic-level favorability to their attitudes toward the EU – that is, the second step of our model.

While several studies have lamented the decline in political, individual and societal trust in Western societies (Dalton, 1996; Foster & Frieden, 2017; Klingemann, 1999; Levi & Stoker, 2000; Newton & Norris, 1999; Putnam, 1995), there is some evidence that European Muslims seem to defy this trend. Political trust can be defined as an individual's confidence that the government would attend to one's interest even if the authority were exposed to little supervision (Easton, 1975). Trust is deemed necessary for the stability and legitimacy of institutions (Gibson, 1997; Klingemann, 1999; Seligson, 2002). Moreover, it is seen as necessary for an institution's survival and proper functioning (Brehm & Rahn, 1997; Norris, 2002; Putnam, 1993). If trust is considered an important pillar of political integration (Morales & Giugni, 2011), then European Muslims, irrespective of their beliefs, seem quite on their way of achieving such a feat as they have been shown in the past to exert greater levels of trust in domestic institutions than all other groups (de Vroome, Hooghe, & Marien, 2013; Doerschler & Jackson, 2011; Maxwell, 2010b).

The majority among European Muslims consists of immigrants. Immigration theories suggest that since immigrants self-select to migrate, they will – once arrived – perceive themselves as being better off than in their country of origin, and perhaps also as having better opportunities in their host country (Alba & Nee, 2003; Dancygier & Saunders, 2006; de la Garza et al., 1996; Maxwell, 2010a, 2010b, 2013; Röder & Mühlau, 2011, 2012; Waters, 1999). This should be due to two mechanisms. First, immigrants in most cases migrate because they believe that conditions in their host country are relatively better. Second, those immigrants that made it to Europe should consider themselves to be the fortunate ones as many who want to migrate to Europe are unable to do so, due to the high entry requirements of the EU.

The result of the relative comparison between country of origin and host country – regarding crucial variables such as the quality of economy, the health system and the political system (Hetherington, 1998; Safi, 2010) – should lead them to be more trustworthy of local and regional institutions. Hence, consistent with previous research, we expect that Muslims in Europe have greater trust of national institutions as an effect of their greater satisfaction with the current economic, health and political situation (Glaser & Hildreth, 1990; Maxwell, 2010b; Röder & Mühlau, 2012).

> *H1: European Muslims – who in their great majority have a migrant background – are more trustworthy toward their domestic political institutions (1a); satisfied with the current economic, health and political situation (1b).*
>
> *H2: European Muslims are more likely to be trustworthy toward their domestic political institutions if they perceive the economic situation to be satisfactory (2a); they perceive the country's democratic system to be satisfactory (2b); they perceive the country's health system to be satisfactory (2c); they perceive their country's governmental actors to be satisfactory (2d).*

European Muslims and EU attitudes

Given recent findings that non-European Muslims often have negative attitudes toward the EU (Isani & Schlipphak, 2017b), the UN and the US, the above-mentioned assumption of higher European Muslim EU favorability seems odd. There is a large literature analyzing the anti-Americanism of Arabs, which might be differentiated along the lines of long-term ideational explanations and rather short-term utilitarian explanations. The former perspective somewhat follows the line of general anti-Western attitudes inspired by the Islamic religion and its conservative traditions (Al-Kandari & Gaither, 2011). The latter perspective highlights individual perceptions of how the US behaves in the Middle East, especially with regard to the Israel-Palestine conflict, and how these perceptions shape attitudes toward the US (Chiozza, 2007; Furia & Lucas, 2006; Tessler, 2003). The populations in Arab countries have also been shown to be least favorable toward the EU and the UN compared to those of other world regions (Schlipphak, 2013).

In contrast, we still argue that European Muslims are more favorable toward the EU than any other (non-)religious group. The reason for that lies in the combination of their (expectedly) higher level of domestic trust, when coupled with findings from the literature on EU public opinion. This literature has for several years now advanced three explanations of why individuals should feel favorable or unfavorable toward the EU: a utilitarian explanation, an ideational explanation and a cue-taking explanation (see, for example, Hooghe & Marks, 2005; DeHoog et. al., 1990).[2]

From the perspective of the utilitarian approach, citizens form their EU attitudes depending on the calculation on whether European integration has larger benefits than costs for them or their respective countries (Gabel, 1998; Herzog & Tucker, 2010). The more a citizen perceives regional integration to be beneficial, the more favorable are her feelings toward the EU. The ideational approach highlights mostly socio-psychological arguments, with citizens having specific psychological predispositions as well as individuals with an exclusive national identity being least likely to trust the EU (Bakker & De Vreese, 2016; McLaren, 2002). The cue-taking approach has been recently separated into two explanatory models: the older models assume that citizens take the EU position of their favored national party as a cue when asked about their individual EU position. As a result, supporters of Eurosceptic parties report more Eurosceptic positions (De Vries & Edwards, 2009), while citizens favoring mainstream governmental parties which are mostly in favor of the EU also demonstrate more favorable EU attitudes (Steenbergen, Edwards, & De Vries, 2007). However, recently these older models have been questioned by an approach which explains former findings by a different mechanism, the transfer of trust (Harteveld et al., 2013, see also Armingeon & Ceka, 2014; Schlipphak, 2015). Viewed from this perspective, citizens trusting their national actors simply transfer this trust to the European level when asked about the EU, about which they do not know enough to make up their mind in an informed way.

We argue here that such a logic of transfer also applies for European Muslim attitudes toward the EU, but that it is not a simple transfer of trust but a transfer of satisfaction. Following the comparison of their host country to their country of origin which already informs their trust in domestic actors, European Muslims (who in their great majority have a migrant background) transfer their degree of satisfaction from the domestic to the European level. This makes sense given that knowledge about the host country being situated in the European context should be available to individuals even with a low degree of political knowledge. Hence, it seems plausible to assume that European Muslims who evaluate their (more well-known) domestic actors according to their relative degree of satisfaction with the domestic political, economic and health system should also evaluate European actors based on the (perceived) domestic situation.

H3: European Muslims – who in their great majority have a migrant background – are more trustworthy toward European political institutions.

H4: Among European Muslims, individuals are more likely to be trustworthy toward European political institutions if they perceive the economic situation to be satisfactory (4a); they perceive their country's democratic system to be satisfactory (4b); they perceive their country's health system to be satisfactory (4c); they perceive their country's governmental actors to be satisfactory (4d).

Data

To test these hypotheses, the article uses data from the European Social Survey (ESS), rounds 1–7, covering the period 2002–14. The ESS is a cross-national, academically driven survey which produces comparable samples of the eligible respondent population, 15 and above, in all countries surveyed. The ESS is a comprehensive and high quality data source which includes a wide variety of indicators of political attitudes for which the questions remain unchanged throughout the survey waves, ensuring survey reliability that allows us to be able to pool the data across years. The pooled samples within the countries surveyed are relatively large, ensuring that a sufficient amount of cases are available to analyze the immigrant population and different religious groups. Due to the methodological rigor of the ESS, we are able pool the data across the seven waves to get an adequate amount of cases to analyze the Muslim and immigrant populations, while controlling for the survey wave in our analysis. Based on criteria of survey representation, EU/Schengen membership and minimum number of Muslim respondents, we choose the following 16 countries: Austria, Belgium, Denmark, Finland, France, Germany, Greece, Ireland, Netherlands, Norway, Portugal, Slovenia, Spain, Sweden, Switzerland and the United Kingdom.

The survey is representative of the overall population but does not claim or is supposed to be representative of the immigrant populations in each country. Since the ESS is not a survey specifically targeted at the immigrant population, there might be problems associated with understanding the language of the survey or due to the surveyor being from the host population, which may cause xenocentric or interviewer bias. Moreover, natives may be overrepresented versus immigrants, or only immigrants who are better integrated into their host societies may be willing to answer survey questions.[3] Despite these potential problems, the ESS remains one of the best sources to carry out a large-N analysis of the European immigrant population, for which comprehensive data on political attitudes is available.

The pooled data contains 207,432 cases without considering any missing values on the dependent or the independent variables. Among these cases 33,794 are classified as immigrants and 3,601 of all respondents identify as Muslim. Among Muslims, 3,434 are immigrants and 2437 are first-generation immigrants.[4] In terms of percentage, around 95% of Muslims in the dataset are immigrants, of which approximately 71% are first-generation immigrants. This further reinforces our application of the immigration literature to the hypotheses generated in this article and demonstrates that one of the basic assumptions in our hypotheses – that European Muslims in their majority have an immigrant background – is empirically valid.

Dependent, independent and control variables

The dependent variable for *H1–2* is the respondent's trust in the national parliament on a 0–10 scale, where 0 stands for 'do not trust at all' and 10 means 'fully trust.' This has been shown as a good proxy for measuring residents' trust in a regime's political institutions. The dependent variable of *H3* and *H4* is the respondent's trust in actors of the European Union proxied by the respondent's trust in the European Parliament (EP) on a 0–10 scale.[5]

We derive the independent variables from the hypotheses discussed previously. First of all, we expect Muslims to be more favorable toward their national parliament and the EU institutions (*H1a, H3*). Hence, we generated a dummy variable separating those identifying as Muslims (= 1) from all others (= 0). The literature has been unanimous that an individual's perception of the economic situation should play a role in the evaluation of political institutions. An individual's satisfaction with democracy, with the provision of health facilities as well as satisfaction with government, should also affect trust in parliament, which is considered conceptually different from government satisfaction. Hence, *H1b, H2* and *H4* relate to the economic, democratic, health and government satisfaction of European Muslims, coded on a 0–10 satisfaction scale.

Regarding potential control variables, we take up two important arguments from the literature. First, if we find European Muslim institutional trust to be highly positive, this would seem somewhat surprising because adherence to Islam is seen in Europe as a major barrier to integration (Foner & Alba, 2008). Some authors have argued that Islamic belief systems are incompatible with Western social and political values, thereby explaining the low levels of EU favorability among Arab Muslims (Al-Kandari & Gaither, 2011). As a result, one could argue that Muslims, particularly those with a higher level of religiosity, might be more unfavorable toward the European level, as a stronger identification with the Islamic faith might lead European Muslims to be more skeptical of any actor representing values like democracy and secularism (especially if that actor can be seen as promoting democracy as a Western and specifically non-Arab value) (Pace, 2009). While we are skeptical of this logic, we include it as a control, as it has been argued to be an important predictor for Arab (Muslim) attitudes (Al-Kandari & Gaither, 2011; Chiozza, 2007; Huntington, 1993). Religiosity is coded on a 0–10 scale of increasing self-perceived religiosity.

Second, from a different but also an ideational angle, one should also take into account that Muslims might feel that they are discriminated against in their country of residence. There exist high levels of anti-Muslim sentiment in many Western European countries (Caldwell, 2009; Helbling, 2008; Strabac & Listhaug, 2008). As minorities, Muslims may suffer marginalization, discrimination and exclusion based on being seen as an out-group with a different culture, identity, religion, race and worldview (Landman, 2006, p. 19; also Crowley, 2001; Sidanius, Pratto, Van Laar, & Levin, 2004). They might face restrictions in accessing economic and political opportunities (Levitas, Pantazis, Fahmy, Gordon, Lloyd, & Patsios, 2007). This may be due to competition they face from the in-group composed of the majority, who wants to hold on to resources and power (Kinder & Sears, 1981; Sherif & Sherif, 1969; Quillian, 1995). As a result of stereotyping and Islamophobia, Muslims in the West may be especially targeted (Ciftci, 2012). In all, the resulting backlash from the host society should in turn make immigrants, especially Muslims, more unfavorable toward their country of residence and its domestic institutions. As a result, they might become skeptical of the political context they are living in and the political institutions of this context which are seemingly unable to prevent or protect them from discrimination. Hence, we also included a variable measuring such feelings. This variable for perceiving oneself as member of a discriminated group is a binary variable, coded 1 if an individual's sees oneself as part of a group that is discriminated on religious, ethnic or sexual grounds and 0 if otherwise.

We also control for other variables expected to have an influence. American politics research has indicated that not only the difference between first generation immigrants and natives but also between first and second generation immigrants might be important. First generation immigrants, per convention, are defined as those individuals who are not born in the country of residence nor are their parents born in the country of residence. Second generation immigrants, in contrast, are born in their country of residence but at least one of the parents is an immigrant. We generated two dummy variables with members of the first generation group or the second generation group coded 1 and all others 0.

Finally, we control for political interest and for the usual socio-demographic aspects. Political interest is the reported level of interest in politics of an individual on 1–4 scale. Education is coded from a question asking for the number of years with formal education, ranging from a minimum of 0 to a maximum of 26. The variable 'female' is coded 0 if male and 1 if female. Age is calculated taking the difference of an individual's reported year of birth and the year the survey wave was carried out.

Models

We proceed in two steps. First, with the help of descriptive statistics along with difference of means tests, tables and figures, we show that European Muslims and non-Muslims differ substantially on our hypothesized dependent and independent variables of interest. Second, we hone in on the factors that specifically determine European Muslims' trust of the national and European parliaments by estimating ordinal generalized linear models (OGLM) in a multivariate setting (Williams, 2010). The OGLM are estimated with country-fixed effects and clustered standard errors, including controls for each of the waves. Due to the ordinal nature of our dependent variable, the first models that come to mind are ordinal logistical regressions. However, these models violated the proportional odds assumption. We also estimated multilevel models with individuals nested in the country of residence as a robustness check but refrained from using it as a main model due to the low-level of units on the second (country) level.

Results

Table 3.1 highlights our main theoretical expectation and empirical finding: European Muslims trust the European Parliament more than any other religious or non-religious group according to ESS data across seven waves.

A summary of all of our variables can be found in Table A1 in the online appendix. We report the means for European Muslims, comparing it to the means for all other respondents. As the latter includes about 98% of the

Table 3.1 Trust in European Parliament among European Muslims and non-Muslims

Religious Denomination	Trust in EUP (1–10 scale)
Protestant	4.66 (n = 33,702)
Eastern Orthodox	4.50 (n = 8,929)
Roman Catholic	4.49 (n = 56,201)
Other Christian	4.23 (n = 2,184)
Muslim	**5.21 (n = 3,127)**
Jewish	4.74 (n = 199)
Eastern Religions	4.68 (n = 737)
Other Non-Christian Religion	4.25 (n = 505)
Belonging to No Religion	4.34 (n = 76,037)

Source: ESS Rounds 1–7 (2002–14).

individual cases in the dataset, we do not demonstrate the overall means of all respondents as they are almost the same when compared to the group of 'all other' respondents. Some interesting findings already emerge. For one, European Muslims seem to feel much more favorable toward their national parliament as well as toward the European Parliament, compared to all other Europeans. Also, and maybe less surprising, European Muslims consider themselves more religious and are more likely to perceive themselves as members of a discriminated group. They are, however, slightly less politically interested than their non-Muslim counterparts. Regarding the socio-demographic controls, we observe that the dataset includes fewer women (46%) for the group of Muslims compared to the group of non-Muslim Europeans (53%) and Muslims in Europe are on average somewhat younger. In addition, given that there seems to be a slight difference in the mean level of education – with Muslim residents being less educated than non-Muslims – we are confident that the sample of European Muslims is not strongly biased.[6] Figure 3.1 further shows the difference in means in the dependent variables among Muslims and Non-Muslims. The bars which show the 95% confidence interval are quite small for non-Muslims because of a greater number of individuals in their sample. They become more visible for Muslim samples but still remain small enough to depict a significant

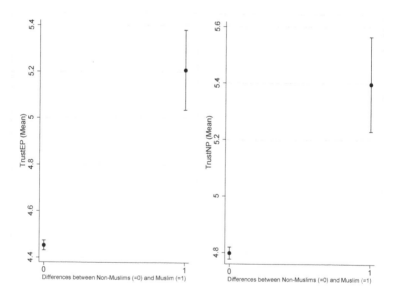

Figure 3.1 Differences between European Muslims and non-Muslims

difference in means among Muslims and non-Muslims in terms of their trust in the national parliament and trust in the European Parliament. This figure shows support for *H1a* and *H3* in the bivariate setting.

To demonstrate that differences exist between Muslims and other groups in the European setting in the independent variables of economic, democratic, health and government satisfaction, we carry out *t*-tests for differences in means. The results of the tests as shown in Table A1 show initial support for hypotheses *H1b, H2a–d* and *H4a–d*, indicating that the mechanism that leads to greater trust of European Muslims in the European Parliament is due to these differences in satisfaction levels in the domestic arena.

The results of these *t*-tests are additionally shown graphically in Figure 3.2. Since none of the bars for the Muslim and non-Muslim means intersect, the differences are significant at the 95% confidence interval. The margin for error for the means for Muslim residents is greater due to the smaller sample size as shown by the size of the bars.

To further probe the factors that determine Muslim trust of the national and European parliaments according to our two-step argument, we estimate two ordinal generalized linear models (OGLM) with logit link functions. The results for which are shown in Table 3.2. These further reinforce our

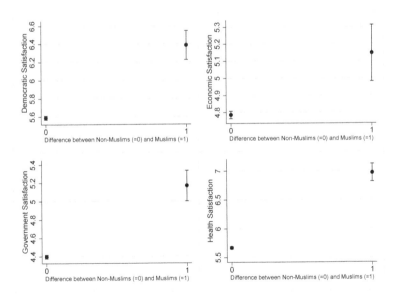

Figure 3.2 Differences in levels of satisfaction between European Muslims and non-Muslims

Table 3.2 Explaining European Muslim citizens' trust in domestic and European
parliaments (OGLM)

	Trust in National Parliament	Trust in European Parliament
Independent Variables		
(*H2a, 6a*) Economic Satisfaction	0.06***	0.05*
	(0.02)	(0.02)
(*H2b, 6b*) Democratic Satisfaction	0.22***	0.19***
	(0.02)	(0.03)
(*H2c, 6c*) Health Satisfaction	0.04*	0.08***
	(0.02)	(0.02)
(*H2d, 6d*) Government Satisfaction	0.28***	0.24***
	(0.03)	(0.03)
(*H3*) Religiosity	0.03	0.02
	(0.01)	(0.02)
(*H4*) Discriminated Group	−0.23***	−0.24**
	(0.07)	(0.08)
Controls		
First Generation	0.08	0.07
	(0.13)	(0.15)
Second Generation	−0.07	0.11
	(0.14)	(0.16)
Political Interest	0.15***	0.16***
	(0.04)	(0.04)
Education	−0.01	−0.00
	(0.01)	(0.01)
Female	0.04	0.11
	(0.07)	(0.08)
Age	0.00	−0.00
	(0.00)	(0.00)
N	2826	2701
Likelihood Ratio X^2	1,302.08***	787.16***
AIC	11,482.14	11,341.79
Pseudo R^2	10.26%	6.54%

Source: ESS Rounds 1–7. Own calculations. Ordinal generalized linear models (OGLM) estimated with country-fixed effects and clustered standard errors, including controls for ESS
waves 1–7, not plotted here. Standard errors in parentheses. * = significant at the 0.05 level;
** = significant at the 0.01 level; *** = significant at the 0.001 level.

previous results that the satisfaction variables are consistently significant in
predicting trust in the national and European parliaments as hypothesized
in *H2* and *H4*. However, regarding the control variables, little support is
found for the effect of religiosity as reporting to be more religious does
not significantly affect trust in the national and European parliaments. Yet,

discrimination seems to play a role, as viewing oneself as being part of a discriminated minority negatively affects trust in the parliaments. Political interest positively and significantly relates to trust in national parliaments and the European Parliament; however, socio-demographic factors do not significantly affect trust in the parliaments.

Summarizing our findings in regard to the hypotheses, Tables 3.1 and A1 as well as Figure 3.1 demonstrate that European Muslims are indeed more favorable toward the national and the European parliaments when compared to other groups (*H1, H3*). The difference is most significant when it comes to attitudes toward the European Parliament, as identifying as a Muslim is the only group with an average favorability score of above 5 as shown in Table 3.1.

Most importantly, the general argument of transfer of satisfaction can also be confirmed. Economic, democratic, health and government satisfaction positively and significantly influence European Muslim attitudes toward the domestic parliament and toward the European Parliament (*H4a–d*). In addition, Table 3.2 seems to also confirm the influence of feelings of discrimination while providing no empirical evidence for *religiosity*. European Muslims who perceive themselves as being discriminated against are more skeptical toward their national as well as toward European institutions. However, Muslims who identify themselves as being more religious are neither more skeptical toward their own parliament nor do they show higher levels of distrust in the European Parliament. Similarly to other control variables, the immigration generation does not seem to matter. However, when we estimate separate models for first and second generation European Muslim trust in the national and European parliaments, as part of our robustness checks, both models as a whole are significant. We also delve more deeply into the potential differences between first and second generation immigrants in the robustness checks section to gain a more comprehensive picture.

Robustness checks

We estimate several additional models (see the online appendix) to confirm that our results are not artifacts of model or case selection. First, starting with the latter, we estimate the same model used in Table 3.2 only for Muslim first generation immigrants and then, only for Muslim second generation immigrants. The chi-square likelihood ratio statistic is significant for both models, showing that the models as a whole are significant for both first and second generation European Muslims. We find that the explanatory mechanisms stay the same: Being satisfied results in trusting national and European parliaments on both levels. However, the experience of immigration matters for the levels of trust in domestic and international actors: First generation immigrants among Muslims demonstrate a higher level of trust than do second generation immigrants. In addition, the perception of discrimination is also significantly stronger among second generation Muslim immigrants when compared to first generation Muslim immigrants. Moreover, first generation Muslim immigrants are significantly more satisfied with the economy, democracy and government compared to second generation Muslim immigrants. These results further substantiate our argument that first generation immigrants are more likely to be favorable toward conditions in their country of residence. We will get back to this finding in the conclusion.

Second, does our baseline assumption regarding the effect of comparing country of origin and host country on one's level of satisfaction with the economy, government, health and democracy hold? To lend more credence to that claim, we calculated for each respondent two additional variables. The first consists of the difference in GDP (per capita adjusted at PPP rates) between country of origin and the host country, while the second represents the difference in Polity IV scores between country of origin and the host country.[7] The baseline assumption expects a positive association between these differences and one's level of satisfaction – the greater the difference, the more one should be satisfied. We calculated two correlation matrices that strongly support our assumption. Differences in Polity IV levels are significantly correlated with political satisfaction – that is, satisfaction with the government and democracy – but not with the other satisfaction variables. In contrast, differences in GDP levels are strongly and significantly correlated to all satisfaction variables.

Third, to check for the robustness of our OGLM models, we estimate weighted ordinal logits with country fixed-effects and multilevel models with individuals nested in their country of residence's GDP – specifically, using Rabe-Hesketh, Skrondal, and Pickles' (2004) generalized linear latent and mixed model (GLLAMM). In either case, these models show similar results in the direction and significance of independent variables in relation to the dependent variables. We also check for a different coding of the dependent variables by coding them as dichotomous variables for trust. The resulting logit model provided similar results. Furthermore, we checked for multicollinearity between the independent variables in our models by using the Pearson's rank correlation matrix, which showed that none of the coefficients were a cause for concern.

Discussion and conclusion

What did we learn so far? In this systematic account of European Muslim attitudes toward the EU, we were interested in the degree of EU favorability and the factors causing it. Our preliminary findings show that European Muslims are very favorable toward the EU – much more so than their counterparts from other religious and non-religious groups. Based on our conceptualization and enriched by findings in the American politics literature, we argued first that European Muslims – who in their majority have an immigration background – are more favorable toward the political institutions in their country of residence as they perhaps compare it with the situation in the country from which they emigrated. Second, by adapting the transfer of trust logic from EU public opinion literature, we expected European Muslim EU attitudes to be influenced by a transfer of satisfaction from their domestic context.

Both parts of the argument are corroborated by our empirical findings. As these findings are robust against different model and data specifications, we are confident that our transfer of satisfaction logic actually explains European Muslims' relatively high favorability of EU (and domestic) institutions. In addition, despite the debate about the incompatibility of Islamic and European values, and political integration, religiosity does not seem to matter among European Muslims. This might have to do with statistical problems following the lack of variance in this variable as many Muslims self-report being quite religious but it might also point to the fact that at least for most of the European Muslims, one's level of religiosity does not play a major role in how one evaluates political institutions. Our data and findings hence indicate that the current lack of social legitimacy of European integration is not because of European Muslims being skeptical toward European political life.

However, we do note that discrimination matters as well. European Muslims who feel discriminated against are more likely to report distrust in political institutions. This is somewhat mirrored by the findings of Erisen (2017) and also by Adda, Laitin, and Valfort (2016), who demonstrate that discrimination hinders political integration of Muslims in the US and in France. Given that perceptions of discrimination are more strongly distributed among second generation immigrants in our data, this might lead to an increase in Muslim (and immigrant) skepticism toward domestic and EU institutions in the future.

Notes

1 This chapter is an adapted version of our article in *European Union Politics* (Isani & Schlipphak, 2017a): Isani, M. and Schlipphak, B. (2017): In the EU We Trust: European Muslim Attitudes toward the EU. *European Union Politics*, *18*(4), 658–677. Copyright © 2017 (Mujtaba Ali Isani and Bernd Schlipphak). Reprinted by permission of SAGE Publications. The authors are grateful to SAGE publishing for allowing us the secondary use of that article. We encourage

our readers to also have a look at the original paper that is accessible via DOI: 10.1177/1465116517725831.

2 Note that this is somewhat mirrored by more general clusters of how to explain trust in political institutions: Some scholars put forward that trust is determined by institutional performance (Foster & Frieden, 2017; DeHoog, Glaser, & Hildreth, 1990; Miller, 1974; Mishler & Rose, 2001), others suggest it is due to personality traits (Gabriel, 1995; Newton & Norris, 1999), while others see it as a result of shared community values (Almond & Verba, 1963; Inglehart, 1997; Ostrom, 1990; Rose, 1994; Mishler & Rose, 2001).

3 One solution to check for such problems might be to compare the demographics of the group one is interested in to the demographics of that group in the overall population, using data from census polls, etc. Regarding the group of Muslim citizens, no such data is available. In fact, even the actual numbers of Muslim citizens in countries is still highly disputed as most countries do not survey residents' religious beliefs or – as in the last census in Germany – used voluntary questions which obviously led to a severe underestimation of the number of Muslim residents. To give still more credence to our findings, we checked the demographics for Muslim respondents in the sample and found them (see also Table A1 in the online appendix of the EUP article [see endnote 1]) to be less educated and somewhat less politically interested than other respondents. Hence, we can rule out that the sample of Muslim residents was biased with regard to education and political interest, which could have blurred our findings.

4 In Table A2 in the online appendix of the EUP article (see endnote 1) we provide percentages of Muslim immigrants in Europe by country of origin. This shows that Muslim immigrants in Europe come from a wide variety of backgrounds reflected in the ESS sample and a specific nationality or ethnicity is not driving positivity toward the national and European parliaments.

5 Other surveys – such as the Eurobarometer (EB) – might offer more and seemingly better questions on residents' EU attitudes, but suffer from a lack of methodological rigor and other problems which have been outlined elsewhere (for a review and several arguments, see Nissen, 2014).

6 See, also, endnote 4. Yet, when comparing the percentage of Muslims in the sample in each European country included in the analysis with PEW data and data from the CIA World Factbook, the Muslim share is found to be about half of the approximate actual percentage of Muslims in the country.

7 The variable for GDP difference is calculated using World Bank Indicator data for 2008, subtracting the GDP per capita adjusted at PPP rates for the respondent's country of origin, from the GDP per capital adjusted at PPP rates of the respondent's country of residence. The Polity difference variable is calculated using Polity IV data from the Center for Systematic Peace from 2008, whereby the Polity score for the respondent's country of origin is subtracted from the Polity score of the respondent's country of residence.

References

Adda, C. L., Laitin, D., & Valfort, M. (2016). *Why Muslim integration fails in Christian-heritage societies*. Cambridge: Harvard University Press.
Alba, R., & Nee, V. (2003). *Remaking the American mainstream: Assimilation and contemporary immigration*. Cambridge: Harvard University Press.

Al-Kandari, A., & Gaither, T. K. (2011). Arabs, the west and public relations: A critical/cultural study of Arab cultural values. *Public Relations Review, 37*(3), 266–273.

Almond, G., & Verba, S. (1963). *The civic culture.* Princeton, NJ: Princeton University Press.

Andrews, R. (2009). Civic engagement, ethnic heterogeneity and social capital in Urban areas: Evidence from England. *Urban Affairs Review, 44*(3), 428–440.

Armingeon, K., & Ceka, B. (2014). The loss of trust in the European Union during the great recession since 2007: The role of heuristics from the national political system. *European Union Politics, 15*(1), 82–107.

Azrout, R., & Wojcieszak, M. E. (2017). What's Islam got to do with it? Attitudes toward specific religious and national out-groups, and support for EU policies. *European Union Politics, 18*(1), 51–72.

Bakker, B. N., & De Vreese, C. H. (2016). Personality and European Union attitudes: Relationships across European Union attitude dimensions. *European Union Politics, 17*(1), 25–45.

Brehm, J., & Rahn, W. (1997). Individual-level evidence for the causes and consequences of social capital. *American Journal of Political Science, 41*(3), 999–1023.

Caldwell, C. (2009). *Reflections on the revolution in Europe: Immigration, Islam, and the west.* New York: Doubleday.

Cantle, T. (2001). *Community cohesion: A report of the independent review team.* London: Home Office.

Chiozza, G. (2007). Disaggregating anti-Americanism: An analysis of individual attitudes towards the United States. In P. Katzenstein (Ed.), *Anti-Americanisms in world politics* (pp. 93–128). Ithaca, NY: Cornell University Press.

Ciftci, S. (2012). Islamophobia and threat perceptions: Explaining anti-Muslim sentiment in the west. *Journal of Muslim Minority Affairs, 32*(3), 293–309.

Crowley, J. (2001). The political participation of ethnic minorities. *International Political Science Review/Revue internationale de science politique, 22*(1), 99–121.

Dalton, R. J. (1996). *Citizen politics: Public opinion and political parties in advanced industrial democracies.* Chatham, NJ: Chatham House.

Dancygier, R., & Saunders, E. N. (2006). A new electorate – Comparing preferences and partisanship between immigrants and natives. *American Journal of Political Science, 50*(4), 952–981.

de la Garza, R. O., Falcon, A., & Garcia, F. C. (1996). Will the real Americans please stand up: Anglo and Mexican-American support of core American political values. *American Journal of Political Science, 40*(2), 335–351.

De Vries, C. E., & Edwards, E. (2009). Taking Europe to its extremes. Extremist parties and public euroscepticism. *Party Politics, 15*(1), 5–28.

de Vroome, T., Hooghe, M., & Marien, S. (2013). The origins of generalized and political trust among immigrant minorities and the majority population in the Netherlands. *European Sociological Review, 29*(6), 1336–1350.

DeHoog, R., Hoogland, D. L., & Lyons, W. E. (1990). Citizen satisfaction with local government services: A test of individual, jurisdictional, and city specific explanations. *Journal of Politics, 52*(3), 807–837.

Diamond, L. J., Plattner, M. F., & Brumberg, D. (2003). *Islam and democracy in the middle east*. Baltimore, MD: Johns Hopkins University Press.

Doerschler, P., & Jackson, P. I. (2011). Do Muslims in Germany really fail to integrate? Muslim integration and trust in public institutions. *Journal of International Migration and Integration, 13*(4), 503–523.

Easton, D. (1975). A re-assessment of the concept of political support. *British Journal of Political Science, 5*(4), 435–457.

Erisen, E. (2017). Seeking refuge in a superordinate group: Non-EU immigration heritage and European identification. *European Union Politics, 18*(1), 26–50.

Erisen, C., & Kentmen-Cin, E. (2017). Tolerance and perceived threat toward Muslim immigrants in Germany and the Netherlands. *European Union Politics, 18*(1), 73–97.

Esposito, J. L., & Voll, J. O. (1996). *Islam and democracy*. Oxford: Oxford University Press.

Foner, N., & Alba, R. (2008). Immigrant religion in the U.S. and Western Europe: Bridge or barrier to inclusion? *International Migration Review, 42*(2), 360–392.

Foster, C., & Frieden, J. (2017). Crisis of trust: Socio-economic determinants of Europeans' confidence in government. *European Union Politics, 18*(4), 511–535.

Furia, P. A., & Lucas, R. (2006). Determinants of Arab public opinion on foreign relations. *International Studies Quarterly, 50*(3), 585–605.

Gabel, M. (1998). *Interests and integration: Market liberalization, public opinion, and European Union*. Ann Arbor, MI: University of Michigan Press.

Gabriel, O. W. (1995). Political efficacy and trust. In J. van Deth & E. Scarbrough (Eds.), *The impact of values* (pp. 357–389). Oxford: Oxford University Press.

Gibson, J. L. (1997). Mass opposition to the Soviet putsch of August 1991: Collective action, rational choice, and democratic values. *American Political Science Review, 91*(3), 671–684.

Glaser, M., & Hildreth, W. B. (1999). Service delivery satisfaction and willingness to pay taxes. *Public Productivity and Management Review, 23*(1), 48–67.

Harteveld, E., van der Meer, T., & De Vries, C. E. (2013). In Europe we trust? Exploring three logics of trust in the European Union. *European Union Politics, 14*(4), 542–565.

Helbling, M. (2008). *Practicing citizenship and heterogeneous nationhood: Naturalisations in Swiss municipalities*. Amsterdam: Amsterdam University Press.

Herzog, A., & Tucker, J. A. (2010). The dynamics of support: The winners-losers gap in attitudes toward EU membership in post-communist countries. *European Political Science Review, 2*(2), 235–267.

Hetherington, M. J. (1998). The political relevance of political trust. *American Political Science Review, 92*(4), 791–808.

Hooghe, L., & Marks, G. (2005). Calculation, community and cues: Public opinion on European integration. *European Union Politics, 6*(4), 419–443.

Huntington, S. (1993). The clash of civilizations? *Foreign Affairs, 72*(3), 22–49.

Inglehart, R. (1997). *Modernization and postmodernization.* Princeton, NJ: Princeton University Press.

Isani, M., & Schlipphak, B. (2017a). In the European Union we trust: European Muslim attitudes toward the European Union. *European Union Politics, 18*(4), 658–677.

Isani, M., & Schlipphak, B. (2017b). The desire for sovereignty: An explanation of EU attitudes in the Arab world. *Journal of Common Market Studies, 55*(3), 502–517.

Kinder, D., & Sears, D. O. (1981). Prejudice and politics: Symbolic racism versus racial threats to the good life. *Journal of Personality and Social Psychology, 40*(3), 414–431.

Klingemann, H. (1999). Mapping political support in the 1990s: A global analysis. In P. Norris (Ed.), *Critical citizens: Global support for democratic governance* (pp. 31–56). New York: Oxford University Press.

Koopmans, R. (2015). Religious fundamentalism and hostility against out-groups: A comparison of Muslims and Christians in Western Europe. *Journal of Ethnic and Migration Studies, 41*(1), 33–57.

Landman, T. (2006). *Human rights and social exclusion indicators: Concepts, best practices, and methods for implementation.* Colchester: University of Essex, Department of Government Human Rights Centre.

Levi, M., & Stoker, L. (2000). Political trust and trustworthiness. *Annual Review of Political Science, 3*, 475–507.

Levitas, R., Pantazis, C., Fahmy, E., Gordon, D., Lloyd, E., & Patsios, D. (2007). *The multidimensional analysis of social exclusion.* Retrieved from http://dera.ioe. ac.uk/6853/1/multidimensional.pdf

Maxwell, R. (2010a). Evaluating migrant integration: Political attitudes across generations in Europe. *International Migration Review, 44*(1), 25–52.

Maxwell, R. (2010b). Trust in government among British Muslims: The importance of migration status. *Political Behavior, 32*(1), 89–109.

Maxwell, R. (2013). The geographic context of political attitudes among migrant-origin individuals in Europe. *World Politics, 65*(1), 116–155.

McLaren, L. (2002). Public support for the European Union: Cost/benefits analysis or perceived cultural threat? *The Journal of Politics, 64*(2), 551–566.

Miller, A. H. (1974). Political issues and trust in government, 1964–1970. *American Political Science Review, 68*(3), 951–972.

Mishler, W., & Rose, R. (2001). What are the origins of political trust? Testing institutional and cultural theories in post-communist societies. *Comparative Political Studies, 34*(1), 30–62.

Morales, L., & Giugni, M. (2011). Political opportunities, social capital and the political inclusion of immigrants in European cities. In L. Morales & M. Giugni (Eds.), *Social capital, political participation and migration in Europe: Making multicultural democracy work* (pp. 1–18). Basingstroke: Palgrave Macmillan.

Newton, K., & Norris, P. (1999, September 1–5). Confidence in public institutions: Faith, culture, or performance? Paper presented at the annual meeting of the American political science association, Atlanta. Retrieved from www.hks. harvard.edu/fs/pnorris/Acrobat/NEWTON.PDF

Nissen, S. (2014). The eurobarometer and the process of European integration. Methodological foundations and weaknesses of the largest European survey. *Quality & Quantity*, *48*(2), 713–727.

Norris, P. (2002). *Democratic phoenix: Political activism worldwide.* Cambridge: Cambridge University Press.

Ostrom, E. (1990). *Governing the commons: The evolution of institutions for collective action.* New York: Cambridge University Press.

Pace, M. (2009). Paradoxes and contradictions in EU democracy promotion in the Mediterranean: The limits of EU normative power. *Democratization*, *16*(1), 39–58.

Putnam, R. D. (1993). *Making democracy work.* Princeton, NJ: Princeton University Press.

Putnam, R. D. (1995). Bowling alone. America's decline of social capital. *Journal of Democracy*, *6*(1), 65–78.

Quillian, L. (1995). Prejudice as a response to perceived group threat: Population composition and anti-immigrant and racial prejudice in Europe. *American Sociological Review*, *60*(4), 586–611.

Rabe-Hesketh, S., Skrondal, A., & Pickles, A. (2004). Generalized multilevel structural equation modeling. *Psychometrika*, *69*(2), 167–190.

Röder, A., & Mühlau, P. (2011). Discrimination, exclusion and immigrants' confidence in public institutions in Europe. *European Societies*, *13*(4), 535–557.

Röder, A., & Mühlau, P. (2012). Low expectations or different evaluations: What explains immigrants' high levels of trust in host-country institutions? *Journal of Ethnic and Migration Studies*, *38*(5), 777–792.

Rose, R. (1994). Postcommunism and the problem of trust. *Journal of Democracy*, *5*(3), 18–30.

Ross, M. L. (2001). Does oil hinder democracy? *World Politics*, *53*(3), 325–361.

Sarrazin, T. (2010). *Germany does away with itself.* München: Deutsche Verlags-Anstalt.

Safi, M. (2010). Immigrants' life satisfaction in Europe: Between assimilation and discrimination. *European Sociological Review*, *26*(2), 159–176.

Schlipphak, B. (2013). Actions and attitudes matter: International public opinion towards the European Union. *European Union Politics*, *14*(4), 590–618.

Schlipphak, B. (2015). Measuring attitudes toward regional organizations outside Europe. *The Review of International Organizations*, *10*(3), 351–375.

Seligson, M. A. (2002). The renaissance of political culture or the renaissance of the ecological fallacy. *Comparative Politics*, *34*(3), 273–292.

Sherif, M., & Sherif, C. W. (1969). *Social psychology.* New York: Harper & Row.

Sidanius, J., Pratto, F., Van Laar, C., & Levin, S. (2004). Social dominance theory: Its agenda and method. *Political Psychology*, *25*(6), 845–880.

Steenbergen, M. R., Edwards, E., & De Vries, C. E. (2007). Who's cueing whom? Mass-elite linkages and the future of European integration. *European Union Politics*, *8*(1), 13–35.

Strabac, Z., & Listhaug, O. (2008). Anti-Muslim prejudice in Europe: A multi-level analysis of survey data from 30 countries. *Social Science Research, 37*(1), 268–286.

Tessler, M. (2003). Arab and Muslim political attitudes: Stereotypes and evidence from survey research. *International Studies Perspectives, 4*(2), 175–181.

Waters, M. C. (1999). *Black identities: West Indian immigrant dreams and American realities*. Cambridge: Harvard University Press.

Williams, R. (2010). Fitting heterogeneous choice models with OGLM. *The Stata Journal, 10*(4), 540–567.

Conclusion
Explaining (Muslim) EU attitudes and their effects: a summary and research outlook

In the introduction to this book, we started from the observation that Arab citizens – who are overwhelmingly Muslim – are quite critical toward the European Union, especially when compared to citizens in other parts of the world. We pointed out at length that we do not consider this skepticism to be due to cultural factors. Or put differently: We did not consider Huntington's famous (or for some notorious) "Clash of Civilizations" to be an explanatory factor here (Huntington, 1993). Instead, we argued that Muslim citizens around the world should be at least as rational as citizens of other or no beliefs. Based on literatures on International and European Public Opinion, on Public Opinion in the Middle East, on Anti-Americanism, and on Attitudes among Migrants, we derived a theoretical framework that proposes a causal two-step process explaining how citizens in general should come to their attitudes toward the international level.

This model, which we termed the "Two-Step Model of Using Heuristics (TSMUH)", has the benefit of combining approaches that have so far been thought of as rivaling each other, the socio-psychological and the utilitarian model of explaining attitudes. In our understanding, actual politics – within the domestic state of a citizen or between the domestic state and a given external actor – first influence citizens' attitudes toward domestic actors. In the second step, they transfer their level of (dis)trust into the domestic actors toward actors on the international level, especially when the international actors are more distant and less known to the citizenry. While the first step of this process includes a rational or utilitarian component, with citizens' taking their (dis)satisfaction with actual political events as explanation for their attitudes toward political elites, the second step embraces the transfer of trust (or satisfaction) which has repeatedly been implied in the literature (see Schlipphak, 2013; Harteveld, De Vries, & Van der Meer, 2013).

To systematically analyze Muslim citizens' attitudes toward the EU for the first time, we applied TSMUH to three highly interesting cases: the EU attitudes among (1) Arab citizens, (2) Muslim citizens worldwide, and (3) European Muslims. This allows us to not only lend credence to the empirical validity of our two-step model but also enables us to provide robust empirical evidence on the factors influencing Muslim attitudes toward the EU worldwide.

Findings

For our first test (Chapter 1), we turned to the explanation of EU attitudes among Arab citizens. Using data from the Arab Barometer, we estimated a structural equation model that mirrors our theoretical two-step model. In the model, we first predict Arab citizens' attitudes toward domestic actors and a well-known international actor (the US) by their individual level of preference for sovereignty and independence. We assumed this level to be the effect of the actual behavior of the US and their own country in international politics. We were able to demonstrate that especially citizens' level of anti-Americanism – but also trust in domestic actors – is influenced by citizens' sovereignty considerations. In the second step of the SEM, we checked whether these attitudes toward more well-known actors actually influence their attitudes toward the European Union. As it turns out, it does so and to a significant and substantial degree. Having controlled the reliability of our findings with several robustness checks, we are confident that the results we found here are valid and reliable.

For our second test (Chapter 2), we used data from the PEW Global Attitudes Project. This allows us to use data for respondents from a large number of countries from all parts of the world. All in all, we are able to include about 13,000 Muslim citizens from 28 countries into the analysis. Most importantly, having that many countries (and also a high degree of country-level variance) in one dataset also allows us to conduct a hierarchical regression model with explanatory variables on the individual AND the context level. Thus, for this test we did not check the actual causal mechanism and process steps outlined in TSMUH but just concentrated on whether there actually is a link from actual politics (that is, a context-level factor) to citizens' EU attitudes. And indeed, there is: The economic relationship between a citizen's country and the EU and its member states – measured in terms of trade relations and official development assistance – significantly and substantially influences citizens' attitudes toward the EU. This does of course not necessarily mean that citizens are informed about these economic linkages. Rather, higher levels of EU ODA and trade relations with the EU that are more beneficial to a specific country should make the citizens in that country to be more satisfied with their domestic actors which again translates to a more positive attitude toward international actors. While this might be good news at first sight, the interesting point about this is that most of the countries included in the analysis have a negative trade relation with the EU which means that in most of the countries, the sum of trade relations with the EU makes the citizens less likely to have favorable feelings toward the EU. We will come back to this at the end of this chapter.

For our third test (Chapter 3), we again tested the causal mechanisms in our two-step model. This time, however, we used data from the European Social Survey to analyze the EU attitudes of European Muslim citizens. Adapting our theoretical framework to the fact that most European Muslims have a migration background, we argued that an actual political event (moving from one's home country to a European host country) should result in higher levels of satisfaction with life, economy and politics that makes European Muslims trust their domestic political actors more. Consequentially, we then expected European Muslims to transfer these higher levels of domestic trust onto the level of the EU. Again, this is exactly what happens, making European Muslims the group with the highest level of trust in the European Union.

Discussion

What do these findings mean for (political) science and politics? In terms of theory-building, our empirical results seem to indicate that our two-step model actually mirrors empirical reality to a high degree. We demonstrate that factors based on actual political events influence citizens' attitudes toward better known actors which then translates into feelings toward more distant actors. Hence, citizens take information shortcuts but these heuristics are again informed by citizens' rational or utilitarian evaluation of actual political events. Attitudes toward international – and most importantly, rather unknown – actors are therefore the result of both rational and socio-psychological problems. In simplified terms – if citizens are satisfied with politics, economy and life conditions, they will like their domestic politicians as well as more distant actors. Research on public opinion toward the European Union (Hobolt & De Vries, 2016; Harteveld et al., 2013) but also toward other regional organizations (Schlipphak, 2015) seems to substantiate that claim.

Yet, there still is a blind spot in our theoretical model that needs to be mentioned as it opens the floor for future research on the topic: the role of political communication. The transfer of trust model – our second step – is based on the assumption that trust in one's domestic actors translates into trust in the European Union. This assumption holds under two conditions: Either the domestic actors are not linked toward the EU and the transfer is just a transfer of generalized trust based on satisfaction with how things are going, or, the trusted domestic actors demonstrate favorable attitudes toward the EU, making citizens that trust their domestic actors simply replicate their EU positions for themselves.

Both conditions have in the past applied for large parts of domestic actors within the European Union. However, the share of Eurosceptic actors among domestic elites has steadily risen over the last years. In fact, they now even form the government in influential countries such as Hungary, Poland and – at least at the time of writing – Italy. Even more importantly, these actors have used their anti-EU position to campaign on the domestic level or to find a common ground for coalition talks between two otherwise fundamentally different political parties – such as the left Cinque Stelle and the right-wing Lega Nord in Italy.

The question derived from these developments is: What happens to our theoretical model if one has to include domestic actors that substantively and aggressively politicize (against) the European Union? Does such a politicization have an influence, first, on citizens' evaluation of actual political events and, second, on the decision-making process itself, as increasing politicization might make citizens to be more aware of the EU, hence skipping the socio-psychological transfer step in our model? Future research – which we are looking forward to participate in – should tackle these questions with even more elaborate datasets than the one we could use here. The answers to these questions are definitely needed to gain a full picture of what factors actually influence attitudes toward the international level.

For our empirical case, the EU attitudes of Muslim citizens, these questions are however of limited importance. The European Union has not been a subject of politicization in countries outside the EU – at least not before the Arab Spring and the electoral campaign of Donald Trump. Being hence unaffected by potential EU blaming from the side of elites, they still have two important implications for EU policy makers – at least from our point of view.

First, EU policy makers focusing on the role of the EU as a norm-diffusing actor – that, for example, connects trade agreements with non-economic conditions that intervene into domestic sovereignty – should be interested in the fact its external behavior actually appears to matter. This is both good and bad news. The good news from Chapter 2 is that the more ODA a country receives from the EU and its member states, the more likely are its citizens to feeling favorable toward the EU. Hence, giving ODA actually pays out. Yet, when it comes to trade, the empirical findings we demonstrate come with a grain of salt. The higher the level of a country's export to – minus it imports from – the EU, the more EU favorable is its citizenry. However, in most of the countries under analysis here, the imports from the EU (greatly) outweigh the exports to the EU, meaning that this context factor rather makes citizens worldwide less likely to like the EU. Hence, connecting these (rather unfavorable) trade agreements additionally with non-economic conditions that might be perceived as intervening into domestic politics seems to be a less successful way to improve the EU's image worldwide. It might be problematic as previous research on the level of elite attitudes toward the EU has shown that it is especially economic and trade negotiation in which the EU is perceived to act unreliably and rather hegemonic (Chaban, Elgström, & Holland, 2006; Elgström, 2007).

Our second implication for policy makers is based on the linkage between the US and the EU, at least in the minds of Arab citizens. Despite the fact that the US is not a member of the EU, the linkage between a great power on the one side and regional/international institutions and international agreements on the other side has been found to be an important factor for explaining citizens' attitudes toward the latter. Johnson (2011), Genna (2017) and Steiner (2018) all have demonstrated that linking a specific international actor or policy to a regional or global power makes citizens evaluate the international actor/policy by their feelings toward the powerful actor. Hence, the European Union seems well advised to distinguish itself from the US as much as possible – especially when it comes to Middle Eastern politics. While this is true for all time points, it seems to be of specific relevance in times of the US government accepting Jerusalem as the official capital of Israel. Given that previous literature has time and again pointed to the robust influence of the Middle Eastern conflict – and especially US actions against countries of the region – on Arab citizens' degree of anti-Americanism (e.g., Tessler, 2003; Chiozza, 2007, 2009; Jamal, Keohane, Romney, & Tingley, 2015), one should expect such actions not to increase US sympathy – and, in consequence, attitudes toward the EU if linked to the US – in the region.

Outlook and research desiderata

In this book, we have analyzed Muslim attitudes toward the EU based on a plenitude of previous literature, a reconceptualization of the explanation model and a plenitude of data. Given that, we are confident that the robust empirical findings in this book give the readers a substantial, wide and concise insight in what drives Muslim support of or skepticism toward the European Union. Together with our previous and current work on the subject (Isani & Schlipphak, 2017a, 2017b; Isani, Silverman, & Schlipphak,

2018), this fits well in the literature on the increasingly relevant topic of external EU perceptions (e.g., Chaban, Niemann, & Speyer, 2018; Chaban, Elgström, Kelly, & Lai, 2013). Still, while especially Natalia Chaban, Martin Holland and their colleagues have made an important contribution in describing external perceptions of the EU worldwide, there are at least three remaining desiderata for future research.

First, we still need to figure out if and how exactly EU politics influence the perception of the European Union. That is, we need to do more systematic research on whether specific EU policies and its effects on third states influence public opinion outside the borders of the EU. Does the Economic Partnership Agreement between the EU and South Africa Development Community (SADC) affect citizens' EU perception in Botswana and Mozambique? And if yes, by which means? This leads to our second research desideratum.

Second, and as already introduced before, we need to understand what causes the politicization of the European Union outside its borders. When do domestic actors in non-EU member states attempt to blame the EU for domestic problems? Under what conditions are they successful with their attempts? Future research aiming to answer these questions may start from research on politicization endeavors within the EU (see, e.g., Zürn & De Wilde, 2012; Hutter & Grande, 2014; Hutter, Grande, & Kriesi, 2016), but will need to move beyond their findings that are based on EU member states only.

Third, and maybe as an even more interesting topic, what are the actual effects of EU sympathy or skepticism beyond European borders? For example, do governments react to their citizenry's EU mood when negotiating or implementing agreements? Does the EU react to public skepticism in a country with which it wants to negotiate? The most pressing item for the EU in this regard seems – surprisingly enough – not that its image might be too bad, but rather too good. Recent calls in the Horizon 2020 research program of the European Commission sketch the puzzle of migrants coming to European countries because they are actually having a too positive view of what Europe is and offers (European Commission, 2018). Viewed from an EU perspective, does it make sense to raise more EU skepticism outside its member states?

We consider all of these three questions to be of highest relevance, to research as well as to European politics. With our work on the EU perceptions of the second largest group of religious believers in the world, we have in our view reached one important milestone – one upon which future research can be based. We are looking forward to further participate in these research endeavors.

Bibliography

Chaban, N., Elgström, O., & Holland, M. (2006). The European Union as others see it. *European Foreign Affairs Review*, *11*(1), 245–262.

Chaban, N., Elgström, O., Kelly, S., & Lai, S. Y. (2013). Images of the EU beyond its borders: Issue-specific and regional perceptions of EU power and leadership. *Journal of Common Market Studies*, *51*(3), 433–451.

Chaban, N., Niemann, A., & Speyer, J. (Eds.) (2018). External perceptions of the EU after the Brexit. Workshop hosted by the Jean Monnet Chair at Johannes Gutenberg University Mainz, 28–29 June 2018.

Chiozza, G. (2007). Disaggregating anti-Americanism: An analysis of individual attitudes towards the United States. In P. J. Katzenstein & R. O. Keohane (Eds.), *Anti-Americanisms in world politics* (pp. 93–128). Ithaca, NY: Cornell University Press.

Chiozza, G. (2009). A crisis like no other? Anti-Americanism at the time of the Iraq War. *European Journal of International Relations*, *15*(2), 257–289.

Elgström, O. (2007). Outsiders' perceptions of the European Union in international trade negotiations. *Journal of Common Market Studies*, *45*(4), 949–967.

European Commission. (2018). *Human factors, and social, societal, and organisational aspects of border and external security*. Retrieved from http://ec.europa.eu/research/participants/portal/desktop/en/opportunities/h2020/topics/su-bes01-2018-2019-2020.html

Genna, G. M. (2017). Images of Europeans: Transnational trust and support for European integration. *Journal of International Relations and Development*, *20*(2), 358–380.

Harteveld, E., De Vries, C. E., & Van der Meer, T. (2013). In Europe we trust? Exploring three logics of trust in the European Union. *European Union Politics*, *14*(4), 542–565.

Hobolt, S. B., & De Vries, C. E. (2016). Public support for European integration. *Annual Review of Political Science*, *19*, 413–432.

Huntington, S. (1993). The clash of civilizations? *Foreign Affairs*, *72*(3), 22–49.

Hutter, S., & Grande, E. (2014). Politicizing Europe in the national electoral arena: A comparative analysis of five west European countries, 1970–2010. *Journal of Common Market Studies*, *52*(5), 1002–1018.

Hutter, S., Grande, E., & Kriesi, H. P. (2016). Politicising Europe: Integration and mass politics. Cambridge: Cambridge University Press.

Isani, M., & Schlipphak, B. (2017a). In the European Union we trust: European Muslim attitudes toward the European Union. *European Union Politics*, *18*(4), 658–677.

Isani, M., & Schlipphak, B. (2017b). The desire for sovereignty: An explanation of EU sttitudes in the Arab world. *Journal of Common Market Studies*, *55*(3), 502–517.

Isani, M., Silverman, D., & Schlipphak, B. (2018). A troubled pair? The MENA region and the EU after Brexit. In N. Chaban et al. (Eds.) *External perceptions of the EU after Brexit*. Workshop hosted by the Jean Monnet Chair at Johannes Gutenberg University Mainz, Mainz, Germany, 28–29 June 2018.

Jamal, A. A., Keohane, R. O., Romney, D., & Tingley, D. (2015). Anti-Americanism and anti-interventionism in Arabic twitter discourses. *Perspectives on Politics, 13*(1), 55–73.

Johnson, T. (2011). Guilt by association: The link between states' influence and the legitimacy of intergovernmental organizations. *The Review of International Organizations, 6*(1), 57–84.

Schlipphak, B. (2013). Actions and attitudes matter: International public opinion towards the European Union. *European Union Politics, 14*(4), 590–618.

Schlipphak, B. (2015). Measuring attitudes toward regional organizations outside Europe. *Review of International Organizations, 10*(3), 351–375.

Steiner, N. D. (2018). Attitudes towards the transatlantic trade and investment partnership in the European Union: The treaty partner heuristic and issue attention. *European Union Politics, 19*(2), 255–277.

Tessler, M. (2003). Arab and Muslim political attitudes: Stereotypes and evidence from survey research. *International Studies Perspectives, 4*, 175–181.

Zürn, M., & De Wilde, P. (2012). Can the politicization of European integration be reversed? *Journal of Common Market Studies, 50*(S1), 137–153.

Index

Note: Page numbers in **bold** indicate tables. Page numbers in *italic* indicate figures.

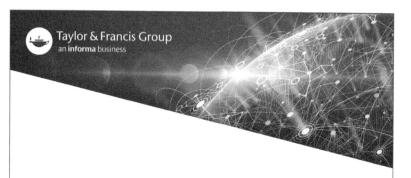